Never Marry a Diplomat

A Memoir

Eva Jarring Corones spent her formative years in Sweden and the United States before leaving for London and then settling in Australia. While in London she completed her Ph.D. in English literature.

In loving memory of my mother Lillan

NEVER MARRY A DIPLOMAT

A MEMOIR

EVA JARRING CORONES

HYBRID
PUBLISHERS

Published by Hybrid Publishers

Melbourne Victoria Australia

© Eva Jarring Corones 2024

This publication is copyright. Apart from any use as permitted under the Copyright Act 1968, no part may be reproduced by any process without prior written permission from the publisher. Requests and inquiries concerning reproduction should be addressed to
the Publisher, Hybrid Publishers,
PO Box 52, Ormond, Victoria, Australia 3204.
info@hybridpublishers.com.au

www.hybridpublishers.com.au

First published 2024

A catalogue record for this book is available from the National Library of Australia

ISBN: 9781922768285 (p)
ISBN: 9781922768292 (e)
Cover design: Gittus Graphics https://www.gggraphics.com.au/
Typeset in Minion Pro

Contents

1.	The Diplomat's Wife	1
2.	The Lund Letters	8
3.	A Conversation We Never Had	14
4.	My Brother Ossian	20
5.	Early Years in Stockholm	26
6.	My Best Friend, Mamma	31
7.	Of all the Ships that Sail the Sea	34
8.	My Swedish Self	41
9.	At Home in Washington	55
10.	National Cathedral School for Girls (N.C.S.)	64
11.	The Intellectual	68
12.	Going Native	75
13.	Abandoned	82
14.	"Sick Tuna"	89
15.	Moscow Interludes	96
16.	Literature and Curries	102
17.	The Career Woman	110
18.	A Major Turning Point: Townsville	121
19.	The Wedding	128
20.	Transition Years in London	132

21.	Anger	139
22.	Moving Downunder	144
23.	Guilt	148
24.	Coping with Two Personae	154
25.	Farewells	158
26.	Relief	161
27.	Becoming Australian	165
28.	Never Marry a Diplomat	172
Afterword		183
Acknowledgements		189

1. The Diplomat's Wife

There was a large house shaded by weeping willow trees with glimpses of high mountains behind it. In front of the house, there was an enormous, deep outdoor swimming pool. I was standing at one corner of the pool. Mamma, as I always called her, was standing on the corner diagonally opposite, about 20 meters away from me. She was dressed up, ready to attend some diplomatic function. Her white dress was covered with sequins and had puffed sleeves and a flowing pleated skirt. She looked like a beautiful angel. I was trying to grasp a yellow rubber duck in the water, or perhaps I was trying to reach out to my mother, when I inevitably fell in. I was fished out by a swarthy male servant also dressed in white and wearing a turban, who carried me to safety. Mamma made no attempt to rescue me or comfort me. Maybe she didn't want to spoil her clothes by getting them wet.

This is one of my earliest memories, and my first conscious memory of my mother. It's from Tehran when I was just over three years old. At the end of 1951, my parents and I had moved to Iran, where my father had been appointed Minister at the Swedish Legation.

At first, I thought I might not have remembered my mother's response correctly. Did she really not pick me up and comfort me? Then I found a short mention of this incident in her diary from June 2, 1952, which seemed to confirm that my memory was correct:

Eva fell into the pool and became sopping wet! Now she will no doubt be more careful.

This is all she wrote in her entry for that day. It seems a very cold reaction. Not knowing how to swim, I must have been frightened and would have needed my mother. Couldn't she have picked me up and changed her clothes? Did she think her diplomatic commitments were more important than being a mother to me? For the first time, I must have wondered whether my mother loved me.

This first memory of my mother encapsulates the view I had of her while I was growing up. To me she was a beautiful woman, the wife of a diplomat, who would spend hours getting dressed meticulously for diplomatic functions or bridge parties and who showed no interest in a career of her own. I also felt that she was keeping a distance between us. It was as if she was afraid to let me, and other people, come too close to her.

Compared to the past, diplomats today are not needed to the same extent as intermediaries between the home nation and the nation of posting. Today politicians and government officials can use quick and convenient air travel to meet in person for discussions, or they can use the Internet as a means of direct communication. It follows that the role and importance of embassies with their diplomats and spouses have also been diminished. However, during the years when my mother was the wife of a diplomat, the 1940s until the early 1970s, an embassy had an important function in liaising between the country it represented and the host country. There was a strict diplomatic protocol to be followed. It was expected that the spouse of a diplomat, usually a woman, would perform certain unpaid duties.

What were some of the duties my mother had to perform during all those years as the wife of a high-level diplomat? Each time they arrived at a new posting, she had to "pay a visit" to each of the other foreign diplomatic wives, whose husbands were of the same rank as my father. Each visit would usually consist of a morning or afternoon tea. Soon after these visits, each of these wives would in turn "pay a return visit" to my mother. On all the visits, a "calling card" would be left with the hostess. My mother's card read: *Mme. Gunnar Jarring, wife of Sweden's Ambassador,* or *wife of Sweden's Minister* when Sweden was represented by a legation rather than an embassy. Mme. was the accepted abbreviation of Madame, the French title of a married woman, French being the language used in diplomatic circles.

There were many other duties my mother had to perform as a diplomatic wife. Each time there was an official delegation from Sweden, my mother would accompany my father on the chauffeur-driven ride to the airport to greet them, and on the delegation's departure my parents would again go out to the airport to say farewell. Much of my mother's time was spent hosting or attending diplomatic functions. When she was the hostess at a lunch or dinner for foreign and Swedish diplomats, she oversaw that her guests were seated as dictated by diplomatic protocol according to their rank. She also had to ensure she provided them with interesting and witty conversation in English or Russian or sometimes French or German. There were also a great number of cocktail parties, which she needed to attend. Often, they were held on the national day of a particular foreign nation or on the national day of the country in which they were posted.

In Washington, as the wife of the Swedish Ambassador, my mother met many famous people, including the Kennedys. There is a press photo of her sitting in the front row, just one seat away from President and Mrs. Kennedy, during a literature reading at the White House which formed part of a dinner in honor of Nobel Laureates from the Western Hemisphere. This was in 1962. In the

My mother (left) with my father next to her at a diplomatic reception in Washington, 1962

photo, Mrs. Kennedy is talking to the American poet, Robert Frost, who is on my mother's right. Interestingly, the JFK Archives mention that my father, Gunnar Jarring, was represented by his wife at this dinner, foreshadowing the role she was later to adopt in Moscow. In his welcome speech, John F. Kennedy commented:

> *I think this is the most extraordinary collection of talent, of human knowledge, that has ever been gathered together at the White House, with the possible exception of when Thomas Jefferson dined alone.*

It's unclear why my father couldn't attend such an important event. I have been unable to find any reference to an important prior engagement in his memoirs or his letters that would have prevented him from attending. It also seems remarkable that my mother attended the event as the representative of the Swedish

President Kennedy (centre left) with Nobel Prize-winning author, Pearl Buck, First Lady Jacqueline Kennedy (centre right) with Nobel Prize-nominee, Robert Frost, and my mother next to him

Ambassador when this role would normally be taken by the diplomat ranked just below him. In any case, I'm sure she would have enjoyed it and would have risen to the occasion.

My mother became a close friend of Julia Helms, the wife of CIA Director Richard Helms, and they were both part of a select women's social group called the Minnows. The picture I have of my mother during those Washington years is of a woman who obviously enjoyed being an ambassador's wife, meeting interesting and often famous people. She was beautiful and knew how to dress well and entertain her guests. As I saw it, she led a privileged, interesting, and enviable life.

However, at various times in my life, my mother would turn to me and say in English: "Never marry a diplomat." I can't remember where or when she first said this, but it seems likely to have been during the Washington years, as I'm sure she said it in English rather than Swedish. Her words certainly had an impact on me. I wondered exactly what she meant by this but can't recall ever asking her to elaborate. Was she being facetious in making such a remark or deadly serious? People have often told me that it was difficult to understand my mother. They never felt sure what she really meant. This is probably because she often displayed a sense of irony, quite foreign to Swedish people, which she perhaps acquired through reading English books. Thus, it is hard to know whether she was being ironic or serious in her warning to me.

Of course, much would depend not just on what she said, but how she said it; how she "delivered" the line, as actors say. Was it said gently, with a wry smile, in which case, she was probably being facetious, or was it said in an imperative tone of voice with the emphasis on "never," in which case she probably meant what she said? The expression on her face when she said it, and how she said it, is lost to me because it was so long ago, but the fact that she said it on more than one occasion suggests that she meant what she said. If she was being serious, then there must have been some dark shadows associated with being the wife of a diplomat. It cannot have been as glamorous as it is often portrayed; there must have been a price to pay. It was only many years later that I would become aware of the cost.

My mother died in February 1999, soon after her ninetieth birthday. I had by then been living in Brisbane for many years. I had no strong desire to attend her funeral, which was to be held in the small village of Viken in southern Sweden. Instead, I felt relieved when my father told me not to rush over from Australia for the service, but rather to visit him in Viken during the Swedish summer, together with my husband and two daughters.

My mother had always exerted a huge influence on me, and

this continued even after her death, despite that I felt I had never really known her. Of course, I knew some facts about my mother's life, and I had my memories of her, but I also had unanswered questions. What did she mean by her warning to never marry a diplomat? Why did I feel such a need to escape from her while at the same time feeling tied to her and being burdened by a strong sense of guilt for having moved so far away from her? Would I ever get to know my mother, or was it too late now that she was dead? Who was this woman who had played such a big role in my life?

Perhaps writing this memoir about my mother's life and my memories of her would help me to better understand her and our relationship.

2. The Lund Letters

Mamma was the youngest of five daughters: Elsa (Essie), Sonja, Harriet (Lalla), Helga (Hella), and Agnes. Their father, Carl Wilhelm Ludvig Charlier (1862–1934), was a distinguished professor of astronomy at Lund University, Sweden. He received two prestigious international awards for his outstanding contributions to astronomical science and has a crater on the moon, a crater on Mars, and an asteroid named after him.

My grandfather's interest in the field of astronomy is reflected in my mother's second name, Agnes Urania. The story goes that her father very much wanted a boy after having four girls and gave up hoping for this after a fifth girl was born. My mother was thus named after the last known planet at that time, Uranus. She narrowly escaped being called Quinta Ultima—the fifth and the last. My mother strongly disliked both of her given names and throughout her life preferred to be called Lillan, which in Swedish means "the little one," a term of endearment often used for the youngest female child in a family.

My parents came from quite different backgrounds. Whereas my mother was the daughter of a professor and the youngest of five daughters, my father was the oldest in a family of eight children and grew up on a large farm in southern Sweden. Instead of taking over the farm as the oldest son, he pursued his linguistic interests at Lund University.

My parents met there, when they were both studying Russian

while also working at Lund University Library. This was in the late 1920s. They were married in October 1932 when my mother was twenty-three and my father about to turn twenty-five. They did not have any children until I was born seventeen years later in 1949.

My father was by then in the diplomatic service and Minister at the Swedish Legation in India. When I was growing up, I thought it would have been unusual and exotic to be born in India. However, my mother had different ideas and flew home to Sweden to give birth to me, as she didn't trust the medical care in New Delhi. There were no more children after me.

Lillan aged 21, Lund 1930

In Brisbane I had some letters that my parents wrote to me over the years, many family photos, and other memorabilia, such as a few of my mother's diaries which contained short entries, many just noting appointments. There were also my father's published memoirs. I hoped that all of these, together with my memories, would help me in my quest to better understand my mother and my relationship with her. Then I suddenly remembered how, during the 1980s and '90s, my father donated many letters and other documents he had kept during his life to the manuscript section of Lund University Library. They were very grateful to receive the donation, as my father, Gunnar Jarring, was a well-known diplomat and linguist, and the papers thus had an historical value and would be of interest to researchers.

My father was born in Viken, Sweden, in 1907 and died there in 2002. In 1933 he completed his Ph.D. on East Turkestan dialects at Lund University. From that time until 1940, he was an associate professor of Turkic languages in Lund.

The year 1939 was to become a turning-point in my father's life. While doing his military service in northern Sweden, he became friends with an intelligence officer. This man later sent for him to act as an interpreter for a refugee who spoke only Turkish. Through this incident, the Ministry of Foreign Affairs in Stockholm was made aware of my father's linguistic talents and sent him to the Swedish Legation in Ankara. It soon became evident that he had other talents as well, and his diplomatic career progressed at a surprisingly rapid pace.

During World War II he was posted to Tehran. In 1946 he set up the first Swedish Legation in Ethiopia. In 1948 he was appointed Minister to India and later to Ceylon and in 1951 Minister to Iran, Iraq, and Pakistan. From 1953 to 1956 he was head of the Political

Department at the Ministry of Foreign Affairs in Stockholm. The following two years, he served as Ambassador to the United Nations representing Sweden in the Security Council. In his capacity as the Council's president, he acted as mediator between India and Pakistan in the Kashmir dispute. My father went on to reach other high posts: Ambassador to the United States (1958–64), and Ambassador to the Soviet Union and Mongolia (1964–73).

In October 1967 he was entrusted with the difficult and thankless task of mediating between the Arabs and Israelis as the Special Representative of the Secretary-General of the United Nations. My father's photograph appeared on the front cover of *Newsweek*, August 17, 1970, with the caption: *Can the Mideast Truce Work? The U.N.'s Gunnar Jarring*. During 1971 he was even a serious contender for the role of U.N. Secretary-General as successor to U Thant, although he consistently explained that he was uninterested in this position. In the first round of votes, he was the only candidate who had no veto against him.

My father was thus a famous person in his time, especially in international contexts. Today, he is best known for his research into the language and culture of the Uighurs—the Moslem Turkic people who live in the Chinese province of Sinkiang. He published numerous works in this field and continued his research throughout his diplomatic career, and especially after his retirement from the foreign service in 1973.

―

Perhaps there was some useful information about my mother in the letters my father had donated to Lund, and it was worth investigating. Thus, on a trip to Sweden in 2015, while staying with friends in Lund, I decided to visit the University Library. I walked up the broad stone steps and looked up at the imposing red-brick facade covered in ivy, with its three triangular stepped towers and large neo-gothic windows. I had often been there when I was a student at Lund University in the late 1960s and early '70s. I thought about how in the 1920s and '30s my parents had also walked up the steps as staff members at the library.

As I went through the heavy entrance door, I came to the main counter on my left. It was large and sturdy, with dark timber panels of a simple design. Surrounding it were columns and an archway, all built of red brick, leading into an adjoining room. I remembered a photo from 1929 showing my father standing behind this very counter, formally dressed in a suit and tie and looking very serious. Now there was another serious young man standing there, but less formally dressed and without a tie. "Could you please tell me the way to the manuscript department?" I politely asked him in Swedish.

Following the directions given to me at the counter, I easily found the department in the basement. I signed the visitors' book and handed it back to the librarian on duty. "Are you by any chance related to Gunnar Jarring?" he asked.

When I gave him my answer, I was suddenly treated as though I were royalty. "Your father was a remarkable person. He often visited us at the library, especially after he retired from the foreign service, and we were very pleased to receive all his papers," he said, almost bowing in front of me. He then proceeded to introduce me to the head of the department as well as to the chief librarian, who were both women of about my age.

After chatting for a while over a cup of coffee and some cinnamon buns, the three librarians directed me to a catalogue, completed in 2008, which listed all the letters and other documents that my father had donated to the library. As I expected, most of these related to his work as a diplomat and to his linguistic research. But imagine my surprise to discover a section entitled "family letters," comprising the correspondence between my parents from 1930 to

1972. I quickly requested the earliest of their letters, written almost twenty years before I was born, and sat down to wait in the small reading room in the basement. In about ten minutes, two large cardboard boxes arrived. Inside these, the letters were arranged in manilla folders in chronological order. They were carefully laid out flat without their envelopes. There were about ten letters in each folder.

My first reaction was to the handwriting. I had assumed that my parents' handwriting would have changed over the years. Instead, I was surprised to find that it was the same as in their letters to me. In the past, letter writing was a way of life, in the same way texting is today. But a quick look through the letters in front of me revealed that it was also quite different. The letters were long, well written, and carefully thought out. Judging by the place names and dates at the top of the letters, my parents were often apart, even after their marriage, which explains the proliferation of letters between them over many years.

There were over two thousand letters which only existed in hard copy, and I had one week in Lund before having to return to Brisbane for work and family commitments. A kind librarian offered me the loan of a camera, so each day I stood up and photographed a series of individual letters after placing them on a dark table covering. It was backbreaking work, and many of the letters were covered in dust, making me sneeze for hours on end. The photographs were then transferred to a USB stick which I took back to Brisbane.

There I began the process of reading the letters and translating them from Swedish into English. I hoped that these letters, together with the material I already had in Brisbane, would help me reach a better understanding of my mother.

3. A Conversation We Never Had

Our present house in Brisbane sits high up on Wilston Hill. It's an old, two-story Queenslander from the 1920s. When my husband and I bought it over twenty years ago, it had been converted into three flats, and it took a lot of time and effort to bring it back to its original state, while at the same time modernizing it. The house is full of furniture and paintings that my parents acquired during their many years in various parts of the world and that I have inherited from them: Persian carpets, Persian prints in gold frames, silver bowls and candlesticks, little jade ornaments, a large, framed photo of myself aged about four sitting in my mother's lap, and a Louis XVI French canapé with four matching armchairs that I remember from Washington. In almost every room, there is something to remind me of the past.

One of the best things about our house is the views, which we never seem to tire of. From the upstairs front deck and kitchen, we can see the planes taking off and landing at the airport; on a clear day we can even glimpse the sand hills of Moreton Island on the horizon. I have a study downstairs but I usually prefer to set up my laptop on the kitchen table upstairs. From there I can enjoy these views when I take a break from the screen and look out the window. With my miniature labradoodle, Milo, asleep at my feet, I am today reading some of the early letters between my parents, which I brought back from Lund.

Mamma was forty years old and had been married for almost

twenty years before I was born. I have often wondered why I was born so late. Perhaps my parents never wanted children and my birth was not planned? I was afraid of the answer and never dared ask this question. Today I have come across many details I have longed for concerning my late arrival. With the help of the letters, I can imagine the conversation my mother and I never had.

Looking back at old photos, I am struck by how beautiful she was. People would often comment on her beauty, comparing her to the Swedish actress Ingrid Bergman, who was just a few years younger than she was. I can see the likeness. My mother had green eyes and a figure which frequently drew admiring glances from men. She was very attractive at every stage of her life, starting from childhood. She kept her good looks into her seventies and eighties, not putting on any weight and maintaining her straight-backed posture. The only change as she grew older was the use of henna to dye her hair a coppery-bronze color.

My mother always spent a lot of time getting dressed and looking into the mirror on her dressing table while doing her hair and applying make-up. In my imagined conversation, we are in our summer vacation house in Sweden, and I am about twelve. As I walk into my mother's room, she is peering into the mirror, carefully applying a bright red shade of lipstick. Worried about disturbing her, I softly ask, "Mamma, why were you married for almost twenty years before I was born? I've always wondered."

She switches her attention away from the mirror and turns around to face me. Thinking carefully, she gives me the long, detailed reply I had always desired, but had never dared ask for. "Well, we always wanted children, but when we were first married, we didn't have much money. We couldn't afford a child, and we both needed to work. Also, I wanted to wait until I finished my master's degree in Russian."

She takes a deep breath and continues, "When my thesis was

almost complete, something terrible happened. I'll never forget it. I was twenty-four years old, and we'd been married for just over a year. I went for a routine medical check-up and was diagnosed with tuberculosis. It was such a shock because I didn't feel sick at all."

She now has my undivided attention. "Then what happened?" I ask.

"In those days, the cure for TB was complete bed rest in a sanatorium in cold room temperatures. You also had to eat lots of rich food such as cream so I gained a lot of weight. It was the only time in my life that I was quite fat. A friend of mine visited and burst into tears when she saw me. I had to have a terrible treatment where nitrogen gas was injected into the space between the two membranes found in each lung. In this way the pressure in the lung increased until it collapsed. After a time, my lungs returned to normal and then I had to have them topped up with the gas. It was incredibly painful! I thought I would only have to stay in the sanatorium for four to six weeks, but I ended up having to stay for over seven months."

"What was Pappa doing while you were away? Did he visit you every day?"

"No, he didn't visit very often. The sanatorium was called Romanas. It wasn't in Lund but near a small town to the north. He couldn't afford to travel there, and he had his work commitments in Lund. He had to work extra hard during this period to pay for my treatment at the sanatorium. And, of course, we had to forego my salary from the library. But we wrote to each other almost every day."

Returning to the early letters between my parents, I find that although my mother tried to keep her spirits up, she was understandably deeply unhappy. In April 1934, she complained: *I have almost been in jail for half a year of the best years of my life.*

In May 1934, there is this:

> *Lord, it's such a terrible disease with always the chance of relapse so that I will probably never be completely happy again.*

There could be no plans to have children for the foreseeable future. In January 1934, my mother wrote to my father:

> *As long as one is taking nitrogen one can't be pregnant. But you are hopefully satisfied with just me.*

In February she was told that she had to endure the gas treatment for a total of three years and wrote from the heart:

> *I would be overjoyed to have a baby instead of being sick for three years without any compensation. Nitrogen and little children don't mix …*

At the end of May 1934, my mother was finally well enough to leave the sanatorium and return to Lund, but she again expressed doubts about whether she would ever be free from her disease, and worried that my father would miss out on being a father.

> *In that case I will get a divorce from you. You are going to have children too. And I probably won't have the strength for it if I don't get better.*

After the three years of the nitrogen treatment were up, the letters didn't mention the topic of children again. Instead, my mother was still worried that she might get sick once more. In her words from February 1938:

> *It's an awful disease and I hate to think that I have it in my body and can never feel completely free from worry that it won't flare up again.*

Reading this, I can completely empathize with my mother. She must have felt not only worried but also very frightened. Antibiotics had been discovered in 1928 but were not in common use. When my mother was ill, tuberculosis was often a death sentence.

After those difficult years, fate stepped in again when World War II was declared. In a letter from January 1940, my mother, who was by then over thirty, expressed her happiness that they didn't have any children to bring up in wartime. There was no mention of a baby in the letters again until 1949. I can only assume my parents made a conscious decision not to have a child during the war. By the end of the war in 1945, my mother was thirty-six years old and would probably have considered herself to be too old to give birth.

The letters give no clue regarding whether my birth in 1949 was planned, and I will never know. In any case, I was relieved to read in the letters that my mother was very happy, but also anxious, at the prospect of finally having a baby. While waiting to give birth in Sweden, she frequently wrote to my father at the Swedish Legation in India. In February 1949, she wrote about the happiness she felt, but also her feelings of anxiety and apprehension about giving birth and becoming a mother.

> *I can't manage children as well as dogs and cats! But we will have to think about how nice it will be in the autumn of our lives to have a being of our own flesh and blood.*

A few years ago, I was shocked when my cousin blurted out: "Your mother would have rather given birth to a dog than to you. She told me so." My mother would have made this comment to my cousin, who was twenty years my senior, just after I was born. After reading the above letter, I no longer feel upset. I now realize that my mother only meant that she was used to dogs and knew how to take care of them, but knew next to nothing about babies.

In several letters from Sweden to my father in India, my mother worried about the pain of giving birth and thought she might not survive. *I myself don't believe in a successful outcome so I am not keen on telling people why I am home in Sweden.* Here she must have been thinking about the fact that she had suffered from tuberculosis and also about her age. In those days it was unusual to give birth at the age of forty, especially for the first time.

In the end, all went well, and I was born in April by Caesarean section. By the end of 1949 my mother returned to India with me, having made the long journey from Sweden to Bombay by freighter via the Suez Canal. I have no memories of our time in India.

4. My Brother Ossian

Throughout her life, Mamma had a succession of dogs. One of them was a little black poodle, called Jimmy, who kept her company in Sweden while she waited for my birth. *He is my black child and is very close to my heart,* she wrote in a letter to my father. Jimmy was with us in India, but when we left in 1951 at the end of my father's posting, Jimmy was flown home to Stockholm where he was placed in the obligatory quarantine. While there, he unfortunately contracted distemper and after much suffering was finally put down, only having reached the age of two. I was too young to remember Jimmy, but my mother often talked about him, and it was clear that she had loved him like a son.

Lillan, Gunnar, and Eva with Jimmy, New Delhi 1950

In June 1952, when my father had completed his posting to Iran, we returned to Sweden so he could take up his appointment as assistant head (and later head) of the political section of the Department of Foreign Affairs in Stockholm. We brought with us a black poodle/German shepherd cross named Ossian. My mother had been given him as a puppy in Tehran by the British owners who had been unexpectedly transferred. His previous owners had decided on his unusual name. It was probably taken from the bard/narrator of *The Poems of Ossian*, believed to have been written by the Scottish poet James Macpherson. Ossian was a large dog, best described as looking like a curly-haired Labrador.

From 1952 to 1956 we were living on Grevgatan street just around the corner from the fashionable street Strandvägen in central Stockholm. As I recall, our apartment building had six storys and would have been constructed in the late nineteenth century. Our apartment on the fourth story was spacious with high ceilings. It had a large open-plan combined living and dining room, three bedrooms, and a kitchen, which was really our family room with a radio and record player, and big dining table. Like most apartments from this period, there was a tiny room just off the kitchen reserved for the live-in maid.

Some of my most vivid Stockholm memories involve Ossian. In my first memory I was about five years old and was looking out through our window, which was still framed by a blackout curtain from World War II; I was trying to catch a glimpse of my mother walking the dog. Our maid was somewhere in the apartment, but I felt alone and afraid as I anxiously awaited their return. I wondered why Mamma had taken the dog yet left me behind.

In the second memory, my mother, Ossian, and I were in the kitchen in the same apartment. I would have been about six. As always, my mother was immaculately dressed, this time in an elegant suit in a light green color with a pearl necklace. The maid,

Birgit, had just placed our lunch of cod soup in front of us when Ossian suddenly made awful choking sounds from under the kitchen table.

When I tried to comfort him, my mother shouted, "Don't touch him! His compact rubber ball must be stuck in his throat. I'm calling for a taxi to take him to the vet." Then she rushed out the door, dragging Ossian behind her into the lift.

I was nervously awaiting their return and praying that Ossian was all right when the front door opened after only about twenty minutes. Ossian raced in, eagerly wagging his tail and heading straight for his water bowl.

When my mother appeared, Birgit exclaimed, "Mrs. Jarring, what's happened?" I was shocked to see my mother's beautiful suit covered in vomit and blood.

"I saved his life in the taxi," she said with a proud smile. "I stuck my hand down his throat and pulled out the ball. In the process he bit me and vomited. I had to pay the taxi driver extra to cover the cleaning costs for his car."

My mother then phoned for another taxi to take her to a doctor as her hand was bleeding profusely and she would need a tetanus shot. She had been seriously bitten when she extracted the ball, so she returned from the doctor with her hand wrapped in a bulky bandage.

The following day, Birgit had the day off. My mother was trying to cook our lunch of sausages and potatoes in a large frying pan while listening to a well-known Swedish pop song on our old-fashioned record player. My mother was very impractical and hated cooking or any form of housework; she was much more interested in dancing around the kitchen while singing along with the pop song lyrics. While she was trying to cook on a gas stove, suddenly a huge flame shot up and her bandage caught fire. Simultaneously, there was a smell of burning. Ossian leapt up from the corner where he had been dozing and started barking. I felt surprised and scared until my mother eventually got the situation under control, putting out the fire and calming Ossian down.

Lillan and Eva walking Ossian, Grevgatan, Stockholm, 1955

Looking back on these two dramatic events, it seems almost inconceivable that they could have happened in our carefully regulated world, but what I particularly remember about them is that they demonstrated how much my mother loved Ossian. She always referred to him as my brother, and he was always with us while I was growing up. As in the case of Jimmy, she looked on him as her son. Ossian was two years younger than me; he died when I was sixteen. Sometimes I think I felt jealous because my mother paid so much attention to him, and she said as much in a letter to my father from October 1955:

> It would be infinitely better to have two children. Now she always wants to monopolize Mamma and can't stand any competition whether from you or Ossian.

Did she love Ossian more than me? I sometimes wondered.

When I was about ten, I was still pondering this question after experiencing the following scene in the Swedish embassy, Washington.

My mother was in the library/family room watching her favorite soap opera on television with Ossian next to her on the sofa. I had just come home from school and wanted to spend some time telling her about my day.

As soon as I was inside the library door and before I had a chance to speak, I was greeted by, "Close the door, sit down, and be quiet. My program has just reached an exciting climax."

After a few minutes of silent television-watching, there was a loud knock on the front door across the hall from the library. I hurried out to answer it, forgetting to close the library door behind me in my haste. It was the postman, who had a special delivery. As I opened the front door, a black shape pushed past me with a snarl. In a second, Ossian had bitten the postman, who was lying on the ground just outside the door, warding off the attack.

My mother rushed out and turned on me, shouting, "You damned idiot!"

At that point one of our maids, Marianne, arrived on the scene to see what the commotion was all about. "Damned idiot," I, in turn, blurted out to Marianne, copying my mother. I then ran down to the creek at the back of our garden and remained there for hours, crying my eyes out. I kept thinking that my mother didn't get angry with the dog for attacking the postman, but with me for letting the dog out. Children have an innate sense of what is just and what is unjust. It seemed to me that my mother's response had been totally disproportionate. Ossian should have been disciplined, not me.

I don't remember that we ever talked about how I felt. I should have apologized to Marianne, and my mother should have apologized to me. Maybe I should have apologized to my mother too for not shutting the door behind me. But nothing was said. I recall that the postman, who was a black American, sued, so my parents had to pay a large sum of money in damages. My mother remained sympathetic to Ossian, explaining that he hated black people because he had been badly treated in Iran before he came to our family. In any event, I asked myself, did she love the dog more than me?

I spent a lot of time with Ossian when I was growing up. He was a great comfort to me when I was left alone while my parents were out attending various diplomatic functions. I can still recall him tearing open his usual Christmas present, a whole Edam cheese, which was wrapped and tied with a bright red bow. I also remember how he would wag his tail and, in the process, clear off whatever happened to be on our coffee table, which was the same height as his wagging tail.

When he died, I felt I had indeed lost my little brother.

5. Early Years in Stockholm

During the Stockholm years (1952–56) when I was aged three to seven, my mother had fewer diplomatic commitments than when we were posted abroad. My father was working long hours at the Department of Foreign Affairs, and I spent the better part of each day at home with my mother. Even though she would have had the time, I don't remember her playing with me or reading to me. Instead, she spent her time listening to the radio or walking Ossian, sometimes with me, sometimes by herself when the maid could stay home with me. Often, she would organize bridge parties with three friends from the Tehran days. As an only child, I was used to entertaining myself, playing with my large collection of stuffed animals, looking at picture books, and using the pencils and notebooks my father brought home from work to make countless drawings.

When my mother had one of her bridge days, I would set up my own small table next to the bridge table and three of my teddy bears and I would copy the bids made by the adults. On many Sunday mornings while my mother was relaxing in bed, my father would take me to the nearby Museum of Natural History, where we would walk around looking at the stuffed elks, foxes, and other Nordic animals. Sometimes we would also visit the open-air zoo at Skansen across the street from the museum.

―

My memories of my mother from this time concern what she frequently said to me. Her words have remained etched in my mind.

As Christmas approached each year, she would tell me: "All I want for Christmas is a good little girl who is kind to her mother." I soon realized that this meant doing what she wanted me to do, and being what she wanted me to be. To her, "good" meant not showing your feelings but having yourself under control. If I cried, my mother would shake her head and say I was overreacting. "What a good little actress my daughter is," she would tell her friends in front of me, making me feel embarrassed. If I tried to explain that I was crying because I was sensitive, she would just laugh at me. If I was angry or upset about something, my mother would threaten to have me locked up. "You're crazy," she would say. I had visions of myself locked in a cell, pleading with the guards to let me out, trying to convince them of my sanity.

As I remember it, I was usually crying or feeling upset because I wanted to attract my mother's attention or wanted her to love me, but instead she thought I was misbehaving. She would then often get angry with me and turn on me with "damned child!" In trying to be "good" on my mother's terms, I became overly dependent on her and felt my life being swallowed up by her expectations of how I should behave. Despite my efforts to please my mother and be a "good" girl, she would often complain: "Why are you so unkind to Mamma?"

Now, once more sitting at my usual workplace at the kitchen table in Brisbane, I wonder whether any of the Lund letters can shed some light on those Stockholm years and help me to better understand my mother.

In several letters to my father, Mamma mentions how difficult I was when I was a young child. In August 1955, she wrote:

> *Since Eva was born, all my energy has been devoted to keeping track of her fluctuating moods and that drains my*

strength! However, this summer I think she has become better behaved and somewhat calmer.

She also comments on my stubbornness, which she calls the worst thing.

By my mother's own admission, she found it difficult to look after me as she was not suited for the task. In an earlier letter to my father from 1951, she had written:

To be honest it's not easy to think with Eva who doesn't leave me in peace for a moment. In any case she is a darling. It's Mamma who is neither suited to nor likes to look after children. Out of all occupations I think the worst one is to be a nurse maid. But, of course, if one had an aptitude for it, things would naturally be different.

This admission perhaps explains why she couldn't deal with any kind of misbehavior on my part, even if it was just typical childish behavior, which most young children display from time to time. Another explanation is that she was used to dogs that can be trained to obey, usually love their owners unconditionally, and will try their hardest to please them.

What about my mother's recurring complaint, "Why are you so unkind to Mamma?" When I now read the Lund letters, I find that this is a similar complaint to those she often made to my father. He could never fully satisfy her great need to feel loved. A recurring refrain in her letters was that he ignored her when they were together and concentrated too much on his work and other people, but when they were apart, he longed for her. She wrote:

It's strange that you think about me much more when I am away than when I am close at hand. Then you don't notice that you often neglect your wife. (February 1949)

My father was a busy man who often had to travel in his work and leave my mother on her own. However, as I remember it, he always tried to be a thoughtful, loving husband to her when at home, but often she still did not feel loved enough.

Throughout her life, my mother would continue to feel insecure and never loved enough, probably stemming from her lack of a mother, especially while she was growing up. From around 1900 until her death in 1956, my maternal grandmother, Siri Leissner Charlier, suffered from an undiagnosed mental illness, which periodically kept her in a hospital in Lund. Some believed it was a form of bipolar disorder, but there is also evidence that it seemed to be brought on or to worsen after she gave birth, so it may have been some kind of postnatal depression. Thus, after giving birth to my mother, Siri was admitted to St Lars Hospital in Lund, and it was decided that there would be no more children. Siri's unmarried sister, Elsa, looked after my mother, who was almost six when Elsa tragically died in November 1914. After that, my mother's older sisters would have taken care of her. My mother keenly felt the absence of her mother due to her constantly recurring illness.

I found a moving letter to my father where my mother made the following comment about Siri:

> ... it is terrible to be ill a whole life and not at all good for the children. You can't understand how it feels to never have had a mother to turn to with your troubles and worries. (March 1941)

In her letters, my mother expressed the hope that she would give birth to a daughter. She had not had a good relationship with her mother, and I imagine she wanted to make up for this by having a good relationship with a daughter of her own. I can understand that she wanted to be a good mother to me, but not having a mother as a role model, she didn't know how to raise a child.

While I was a young child in Stockholm, a tactic my mother often used was the threat, "You'll get your punishment one day," if she thought I had been unkind, uncontrolled, and trying to escape from her great influence over me, instilling a terrible sense of guilt in me and making me wonder what form this future punishment would take. I believed that I had to please her and act in accordance with her wishes. If I didn't do this, I would feel guilty.

It was during these early years of my childhood that I would have recurring nightmares where I was chased by a wild animal: a wolf, panther, lion, or bear. In these dreams I would try to escape by climbing up onto the top of a wardrobe. I always woke up when the beast started sniffing around my feet and was about to take a bite. I wonder if the dreams meant I was afraid of my mother's anger if she thought I had misbehaved? Or perhaps it was the punishment with which she threatened me that I feared and that took on the shape of wild beasts.

I also sometimes wonder if my irrational fear of birds, which I've suffered from since I was a young child, could stem from a fear of my mother's anger. Some early photos show her wearing a hat with large feathers, of the sort that was fashionable in those days. It may have been one of the hats she proudly told her friends she had bought with the Swedish government money she regularly received for child support. Did I fear that she would, birdlike, fly at me in a rage? Did she perhaps even do so on some occasion that I have stored in my subconscious mind? No one has ever been able to explain my bird phobia, which was so acute at an early age that I was terrified of even a lone feather not attached to a bird and refused to sleep on a pillow filled with down.

Today I feel very uncomfortable if I am eating in a restaurant or café and there are birds around. I worry that they will fly at me, flapping their wings.

6. My Best Friend, Mamma

Looking back on those Stockholm years, it seems the relationship between my mother and me was complicated and often difficult. However, we also spent a lot of time together and were close. This continued during the two years we spent in the village of Larchmont, 29 kilometers northeast of midtown Manhattan, from where my father would commute to New York in his role as Sweden's Ambassador to the United Nations from 1956 to 1958. I was then aged seven to nine.

It was during these years that I felt closest to my mother. I was so tied to her that I couldn't go to sleep until she and my father came home from some diplomatic function or other party. They were often out until late at night. I would lie in my room with my heart pounding, straining to hear their car coming up the driveway. Sometimes I felt not only alone but scared, and would wake up the current maids, who had rooms in a different part of the house. They were often annoyed with me, and once even gave me a sleeping tablet as they were desperate for me to leave them alone so that they could go back to sleep.

When my parents finally came home, I was usually still awake. My mother would let me sleep next to her in the king-size bed in her room, where our dog Ossian had also been anxiously waiting for her return and where he always stayed during the night. I think she realized that once in her room, I would at last fall asleep.

My parents always slept in separate bedrooms. This was because my father liked to get up at around 6 a.m. or earlier to do some reading and writing, while my mother was an evening person who liked to sleep in until around 8 a.m. It's also a fact that my father was a loud snorer even when he was young, so their sleeping arrangements were for practical considerations and not a sign of an unhappy marriage.

In a diary entry from Stockholm in October 1955, my mother commented:

> *It would be ideal to have two children sleeping in the same room in the evenings. Now she always feels alone and abandoned if Mamma is not in her room at 8 p.m. in the evening! And of course, I can't comply with this—not now nor in the future.*

It was only during the Larchmont years that she succumbed to my wish to stay in her room, and these were also the years that I was most tied to her. I must have stayed in her bed most nights, as I have no recollection of ever falling asleep and waking up in my own bed. In Stockholm and Washington, I stayed in my own room, which was next door to my mother's and Ossian's. During those Larchmont years my mother would often ask me, "Who is your best friend?" and I would dutifully answer, "You are," knowing that this was the response she wanted from me.

My close ties to my mother were probably intensified by the fact that I never bonded with any of the series of nannies and maids who looked after me while I was growing up. This was because none of them stayed with us for very long. Some left due to illness. Some only wanted the experience of working abroad for a short time. Others were with us for a year of training before they returned to their "domestic training" schools in Sweden. When I was a baby in India, my father's unmarried sister Greta looked after me for a time after Sister Bertha, my first nanny, had been forced to return home to Sweden due to ill health. Greta was always one of my favorite aunts, but I was unfortunately too young to remember her from the India days.

Reading some short entries in my mother's diaries, I found evidence that my mother was more involved in looking after me during the Larchmont years than in Stockholm or later in Washington. I discovered that she had walked me to and from school in Larchmont on most days and that she had helped out as a class mother when I was in grade 3. She also took me to swimming lessons at the Larchmont beach on Long Island Sound. I hadn't remembered any of this before reading those diaries.

7. Of all the Ships that Sail the Sea

Lillan and Eva crossing the Atlantic in 1960

I can trace my lack of physical courage back to my mother. She was overly protective. I remember feeling embarrassed when she wrote a note to my grade 4 physical education teacher saying that I was not allowed to do somersaults as I might break my neck. She also tended to pass her own fears on to me. I can trace my intermittent fear of thunderstorms, car travel, and flying as being her phobias, which I have inherited. I can still see her nervously sitting in the back seat with clammy hands when traveling by car. My fear of flying has fluctuated over the years. At a stage when I really enjoyed flying, my mother turned to me and said, "Which part do you think is most frightening: the take-off or landing?", making me think that both parts involved an element of danger and making me feel afraid. Even today, when I am in a situation that could potentially pose some form of danger, it's as though I can hear my mother's voice in my head, issuing a warning to me.

Strangely enough, I was never influenced by her fear of sea travel. During our six years in Washington, my mother and I would travel back and forth to Sweden by ship for our annual three-month summer holiday in Sweden during June to August. We would always travel on the Swedish American Line's MS *Kungsholm* or her sister ship the MS *Gripsholm*, which crossed the Atlantic from New York to Gothenburg, the voyage lasting about seven days. During our crossings, my mother would often talk about the terrible fate of the *Titanic*, especially during the compulsory lifeboat drills when we were all huddled on the top deck, dressed in warm clothes and life jackets. We traveled first class and were always seated at the captain's table, where on some of our trips we were joined by Hokan Bjornstrom Steffanson, a Swedish businessman who survived the sinking of the *Titanic* in 1912 by jumping at the last minute into a lifeboat. When Steffanson was on board with us, my mother felt safe because she (erroneously) believed that it was statistically impossible for him to find himself on a sinking ship twice.

During those boat trips, I spent a lot of concentrated time with my mother. We shared a luxurious stateroom and spent most of the day together. Our daily routine included breakfast in bed, reading on deck chairs, lunch in the first-class dining room, an afternoon movie in the auditorium, dressing for dinner, pre-dinner drinks in the lounge, and dinner followed by some form of entertainment.

Sometimes we also took the lift down to D-deck, well below the surface of the ocean, for a swim in the pool. For me this was a frightening experience. Despite the ship being equipped with stabilizers to keep it on an even keel, the crossings were often quite rough and the water in the swimming pool would slosh from side to side, making it difficult to swim. I would usually cling to the edge of the pool while my mother made a few attempts to swim across it.

I was living the life of a retiree on a luxury cruise ship. Many of our fellow passengers were in fact quite elderly, and I was usually the only child at the captain's table. I didn't mind this, as I was used to the company of older people. My parents were forty years older than me and tended to have friends their own age. These friends either didn't have children or their children were already grown up.

During my childhood, my mother often wanted to show me off in front of people. She told me that I had a great-aunt who was a famous opera singer at the Royal Palace of Stockholm, and that perhaps I had inherited her musical talent. I could sing in tune, but my voice was in no way exceptional. However, while I was a child, I was often made to sing in front of visitors, which I reluctantly did from behind the living room or dining room curtains.

On one of our trips across the Atlantic, one evening after dinner my mother made me perform in front of hundreds of passengers in the first-class lounge. I would have been about ten. I don't remember her asking me to do it. It was just expected of me and, as always, I wanted to please her. I sang "Catch a Falling Star," the song made popular by Perry Como, and another song in Swedish popular at the time. I don't remember feeling embarrassed or scared to perform, but I do remember my mother telling me how the following day many people had congratulated her on her daughter and how proud she felt. I think she added that she thought the pitch of my voice had been too high. She was hard to please.

My mother was also vain. Although she was near-sighted, she

refused to wear glasses. Sometimes she wore prescription sunglasses which she thought made her look glamorous. She looked much younger than her age and didn't want people to know that she was an older mother. Her solution was to keep me looking as childlike (and acting as childish) as possible. Thus, up to the age of fifteen, I was dressed in little girls' dresses with bows and flounces and was still playing with dolls while my friends were becoming increasingly sophisticated and interested in boys. This was, of course, another way for my mother to tie me to her when I should have been on the way to becoming an independent person.

One of the last Atlantic crossings we took together was in June 1963. It was the evening of the captain's dinner, a farewell dinner held on the last night of the voyage. In our stateroom, my mother took even greater care than usual with her appearance in preparation for the dinner. She was no doubt hoping for some compliments from the men at our table and for a dance with the captain after dinner. She spent what seemed like hours peering into the dressing table mirror and puckering her mouth while concentrating to apply her lipstick. Although I had recently turned fourteen, I was not allowed to wear make-up, not even the tiniest amount of lipstick, and the best I could do to prepare was to slick back my hair with water. My mother quickly commented that this was not an improvement.

When we took our seats at the captain's table, Countess Trudy Knuth-Winterfeldt and her daughter, Isabel, were already seated. This was one trip where I was not the only young person at the table. Count Knuth-Winterfeldt was Denmark's Ambassador to the U.S.A., but like my father, he did not have the time to travel by boat and instead always traveled by plane. On her annual trips to Denmark, the countess always brought her three Afghan hounds with her on the ship. They were housed in large cages outside on the aft deck, and I was allowed to visit them with the countess and to pat their long, silky coats. Due to the quarantine requirements in Sweden, poor Ossian had to stay in a kennel in the States while we were away, but the regulations in Denmark must have been less strict.

We were soon presented with an elaborate menu comprising many dishes: Caviar Malossol, Turtle Soup Lady Curzon, Cold Salmon Bellevue, and Roast Pheasant Souwaroff. As usual I had consumed a whole bowl of peanuts while my mother had a pre-dinner drink in the lounge, so I wasn't overly hungry. And I wouldn't be eating the turtle soup as it reminded me of my pet turtles, called Eva and Ossian, who had died recently. However, the dessert, Bombe Kungsholm, immediately caught my attention. The "Bombe" turned out to be a kind of baked Alaska in a round shape with a sparkler on top, brought in from the kitchen on separate plates, one for each table. The plates were carried in shoulder-high by the waiters, who sang the "Kungsholm Song" before depositing their plates on the table. The waiters enthusiastically and loudly sang the lyrics of the song, some in tune, others not:

> *Of all the ships that sail the sea*
> *The ship for me is the Kungsholm.*
> *More than just an ocean liner*
> *Not a ship that's built is finer.*
> *We play, we sing, we dance and dine*
> *With a glass of wine and a girl.*
> *So let's make our goal*
> *Just one more "skaal"*
> *To the good Kungsholm.*

After the gala dinner, there was dancing in the first-class lounge, which the captain attended for a while before returning to the bridge. I can still see him walking over to Countess Knuth-Winterfeldt to ask her for a dance when at the last minute he said: "No, I think I'll ask *Miss* Knuth-Winterfeldt." I identified with Isabel, who was only a few years older than me. It was as though the captain had chosen *me* to dance instead of *my* mother, despite her elaborate attempts at making herself attractive. I had reached an age where I could assess my mother objectively.

Lillan and Eva at the captain's table on the Kungsholm, 1963

My mother's vanity was obvious to me on those trips across the Atlantic, but throughout her life there were other examples too. To take one, I will never forget my mother's visit to London in 1983. My husband and I had been living there for several years and our daughter Celia had been born there at the end 1982. Mamma was staying at a hotel near us and on the way over to see her, I felt very excited about introducing her to her first grandchild—but her reaction was not what I expected. When I entered her hotel room, instead of immediately admiring Celia, she continued looking at herself in the mirror. Perhaps she was trying to persuade herself that she still looked young and beautiful at seventy-four and not at all like a grandmother. I felt disappointed in her.

My mother's vanity not only affected me while I was young, but also in later life. I didn't like the fact that she spent so much time looking into the mirror, applying make-up, and deciding which striking, often colorful outfits and pieces of jewelry she would wear on that particular day. It may be that I felt that this was another example of her neglecting me, but I also felt it was time wasted on frivolous and attention-seeking behavior. I think early on I decided I did not want to copy her in this regard, and this probably explains why I have never worn a lot of make-up or jewelry, and why I like to dress simply and comfortably.

In order to be vain, you also must feel sure that you are good-looking; I have seldom felt completely confident in that regard. I believe a mother should help to boost a daughter's self-confidence, but my mother's comments and behavior often had the opposite effect. I still remember her words to the mother of one of my American classmates, who had come to pick up her daughter from our house in Washington. While observing my friend and me, my mother said: "My daughter is not so fair." It could be that my mother meant that my hair was not as blonde, but I had the distinct feeling that she meant the other girl was prettier.

During my early teenage years, when girls tend to be increasingly sensitive about their appearance, my mother turned up one day carrying a wooden rod which she said was for doing back exercises which would help improve my bad posture. Perhaps she meant well, but it made me feel awkward and unattractive.

My only memory of my maternal grandmother, Siri, is visiting her in the mental hospital in Lund together with my mother when I was about six. "You are ugly, but I like you anyway," was my grandmother's greeting to me. I don't know what made her say this as, judging by the many photos I have seen of myself from my early childhood, I was quite a pretty child. In any case, I recall feeling upset but my mother said nothing and didn't try to comfort me.

Why did my mother behave in this way? Did she just speak her mind without thinking about the effect her words might have on me? Was she unable to imagine how her behavior or lack of sympathy would affect me?

8. My Swedish Self

Eva in Swedish national costume, Stockholm, 1955

The first time my mother and I found ourselves on board the MS *Kungsholm* on our way across the Atlantic was in October 1956, after my father had been appointed Sweden's Ambassador to the

United Nations. When we arrived in New York, my father was waiting for us on the pier looking very tall and happy to see us. My father always chose his words carefully, saying the right thing depending on what the occasion demanded, in accordance with his well-practiced role as a diplomat. I will never forget his words of welcome. "You are now standing on American soil," he said as he looked down at me from his great height. "But you will never forget your own country or your own language."

My father had a deep love of Sweden and Swedish traditions. He thought it was important to keep in touch with the country he was representing abroad by spending his vacations from various diplomatic posts in his home country, and he also wanted me to have a strong connection with Sweden. Thus, from the age of two, I spent almost every summer of my childhood and adolescence in the small village of Viken, meaning "the bay" and pronounced *Veeken* with the accent on the first syllable. It is situated in southern Sweden on the coast along Oresund, the sound between Sweden and Denmark, which links the Baltic Sea and the North Sea. We always went to Viken because my father was born there, and he felt deeply connected to the place throughout his life. He came from a very large family and had about sixty first cousins, most of whom lived in the Viken area. Thus, when we walked around the village, everyone knew who we were and many of the people we met were in fact our close relatives.

At the end of 1990, my parents settled into retirement in Viken. By that time, I was living in Australia, but would come for a visit every one or two years. During their retirement my parents were still living in our first house in Viken, which was originally meant to be just a summer home for our holidays from the diplomatic service. Now the house was crammed full of books, paintings, and ornaments collected during many varied diplomatic posts abroad. The house was impractical, with a kitchen and bathroom that had not been renovated since being installed in the late 1950s, and it was difficult and expensive to heat it in the cold Swedish winters. Nonetheless, my parents loved living there.

I especially remember one of my visits from Australia when my father was in his nineties. It was July 1999, the summer after my mother died. My father and I were enjoying the unusually warm and sunny Swedish summer sitting on the front veranda, which was paved with flagstones and surrounded by meter-high hollyhocks as well as roses and snapdragons. We were relaxing in comfortable garden chairs with a glass-top table between us, on which there was a little Swedish flag next to our drinks: a whisky for my father and a glass of Harvey's Bristol Cream for me.

While we were chatting, my father told me how he had always planned to eventually settle in Viken: "I was never tempted to settle abroad after retirement. Some of my colleagues have done so because they considered the Swedish climate to be too harsh and the winters too long and dark. I've never been able to understand them. I am so attached to Viken."

"I've always loved Viken too," I said. "I always look forward to visiting you here. I love walking down the main street with its old houses with thatched roofs and beautiful gardens. It's just such a pity that many of the small shops on the main street have closed. Remember the grocery store that you always went to? The one with sausages made on the premises and delicious Danish cheeses. Why did they close?"

"There was too much competition from the big food chain store on the other side of the highway. That's why Gustavsson's store closed too."

"I remember that store well. You could buy not only food but also wooden shoes with various hand-painted designs. I still have the pair I bought a few years ago—decorated with cats and flowers."

My father continued to talk about Viken as it was in the past, about its many different shops, dairies, blacksmiths, and shoemakers as well as many hotels and restaurants. He called it "simply a community full of life." This is also how I remember it. During our summer holidays in the 1950s and '60s, Viken became even more lively through an influx of visitors from Denmark and other parts of Sweden, who wanted to enjoy a holiday at the beach. In my memory of those summers, the sun was always shining, and walking down the main street was a bit like being in Willy Wonka's chocolate factory in the book by Roald Dahl. Starting out from the church and walking south, on the left there was a bakery (one of the few shops still in existence) with green marzipan frogs, then Persson's news agency where you could buy salty liquorice in the form of coins and cats. On the right was "Vibo," with home-made ice cream in waffle cones, and almost opposite "Zermans" which competed with them all in what it offered.

In my mind's eye I can clearly see Viken's Hotel on the main street with its heart-shaped sign proudly displaying its name. This was where my parents entertained former U.S. President George Bush Senior when he visited them in Viken in July 1971. Bush was then U.S. Ambassador to the United Nations, and my father often met him on his trips to New York during his time as U.N. mediator in the Middle East. I have several photos from this visit. My favorite among them is one of my mother standing close to the handsome Ambassador Bush while holding on to his arm with a pleased and flirtatious look on her face.

Running parallel to the main street is the beach, which during my childhood was full of sand rather than today's shingle. The water was clean and inviting, and as you were swimming you could look across the sound to Denmark and far to the left even catch a glimpse of Hamlet's castle in Helsingør (Elsinore). On my annual visits to Viken as a child, I never ceased to feel excited by the sight of the ancient, dark-brown timber windmill and the white

Lillan and Gunnar with George Bush Senior, Viken, July 1971

church steeple on the horizon as we made our way by taxi from Helsingborg, the nearest big city. I felt I was coming home. When I now visit Viken as an adult, I am still thrilled when I catch sight of these two landmarks in the distance as I approach the village.

When I think back to those past summers in Viken, I see my mother riding her red bicycle down to the beach for her daily swim, whatever the weather. She would keep track of these swims in a notebook and would reach a formidable number by the end of the summer. Going for a swim in Sweden is quite a different experience to that in Australia. The Swedish summers are usually cold by Australian standards. You don't go in the water to cool off but rather to enjoy the exhilarating feeling when your circulation has been boosted from spending a short time in the cold waves. Your body feels warm and tingling when you emerge.

My father didn't swim, or at least not very often. Instead, his exercise consisted of mowing the lawn, immaculately dressed in a grey suit and tie, always the diplomat even when on vacation. My parents spent a lot of time reading and having a drink or dinner with their friends.

My memories of my early Stockholm years are strongly connected to my mother and having to play by myself, whereas my memories of Viken are linked to my relationship with other people who were my friends, and to my extended family. I often only saw my parents at mealtimes. We had a big brass bell or maybe a string of three bells, which would previously have hung around the neck of a camel, and which my parents brought back to Sweden from a trip abroad before I was born. This bell could be heard for some distance. A maid, or my mother, would stand in the garden and ring the bell to summon me back home from somewhere in our neighbourhood for lunch at 12 and dinner at 6.

Even as a young child, I experienced an enormous sense of freedom in Viken. It was a safe environment where everyone knew everyone and where there were few cars on the road. I was allowed to walk or ride my bike around the village without adult supervision, which was quite different to spending a lot of time with my mother inside the Stockholm apartment. I would often play outside our house with the many neighbourhood children, who were around my age. In those days our street was just a dirt track and there was a large empty lot with tall grass where we used to play hide-and-seek.

One of my favorite pastimes was riding my bike to visit "Gardener Paulsson," who lived on a small farm just beyond the windmill, where he grew fruit and vegetables that he would sell to the villagers. He was a handsome, middle-aged bachelor who loved the animals on his farm: several hunting dogs, polecats (which were kept in a cage, and which gave off a terrible smell), hens and roosters, and the working horse, Molly. I was sometimes allowed to ride bareback on old Molly while she pulled an old-fashioned plough carefully steered by Paulsson walking behind it. Once Paulsson gave me a little yellow hen and a much bigger black rooster to look after during our summer vacation. I named them Goldie and Black Peter. They were promptly installed in an old hut at the back of our garden and were also given a small, caged area outside the shack. I think my parents thought that looking after the birds would be a good way for me to overcome my bird phobia. However, it never had the desired effect. I was terrified every morning when I had to enter the shack to feed the birds and clean up after them. I was very happy to return them to Paulsson at the end of the summer.

My friend Agneta was my age and had red hair and freckles like Astrid Lindgren's *Pippi Longstocking*. For about six years, her parents, Stig and Marta Groth, rented the same small cottage across the road from us for their annual summer holiday. From the age of about nine to fourteen, I spent much of my time in Viken playing with Agneta, usually over at her house or outside somewhere in the village. While my parents were reading, writing letters, or generally relaxing at home often with a drink or two, I enjoyed being with the close-knit Groths, who welcomed me as part of their family, which was so different to my own. Mr. Groth was a chef providing meals for the staff of a large company in Helsingborg. Mrs. Groth was a good cook too and prepared delicious snacks for us. She also had a sewing machine which she would use to make elaborate outfits for our Barbie dolls.

While they were posted abroad, my parents could always rely on having chauffeur-driven cars at their disposal. For this reason, they never owned a car of their own or even bothered to get a driver's license. This meant that during the Viken holidays, we had to depend on relatives or friends to help us when we needed a car, for example when shopping for items that couldn't be found in the local shops. Sometimes we would have to take the bus or occasionally a taxi into Helsingborg. The lack of our own transport also meant that we couldn't easily visit the many scenic spots in the Viken area. The Groths, on the other hand, would go on evening drives to picturesque places and often asked me to accompany them. On one memorable occasion, Agneta called to me from across the road separating our two houses: "We're going for a drive. Do you want to come?"

I happily accepted the offer. It was one of those long evenings in the early summer when the sun would not set until 11 p.m. We drove through the bright yellow fields of rape alternating with birch forests, with the dark blue sea around every corner. I felt lucky and excited to be a part of this experience. We drove to a beach to the south of Viken, where there were still concrete bunkers from World War II. These had been built to protect the Swedish coastline from the Germans across the sound in occupied Denmark. Mr. and Mrs. Groth sat down on a bench to admire the view.

"Let's play hide and seek among the bunkers," I suggested to Agneta and her sister, Barbro.

I had found a good hiding place when I suddenly felt a sharp pain. I had leaned forward and had managed to get an iron spike from a bunker into my throat. When I looked at my hand after touching my throat, it was covered in blood. In a panic, I first thought the spike had penetrated so deep that I would be unable to call out to the others, but I soon managed to shout for help. The Groths rushed me to the hospital in Helsingborg where I had stitches and was given a tetanus shot.

I must have been a very clumsy, accident-prone child because the following summer Agneta, Barbro, and I were out on a long bike ride when I fell off my bike and rolled into a ditch. This was a less serious accident than the previous summer, resulting in just some bruises and scratches, and we managed to ride our bikes back to Viken. Mr. Groth again kindly drove me to the hospital.

What strikes me about these two accidents is that neither of my parents came with us to the hospital. I have no memory of how they reacted when we got back to Viken. Perhaps they weren't home? Maybe they were on a trip away from Viken or had been invited out for dinner leaving a maid in charge? Or were they home but happy to leave me in the care of Mr. Groth? I don't remember my mother being there to comfort me. Did I again wonder whether she loved me?

For many years my paternal grandparents owned a large farm on the outskirts of Viken. In 1948 they retired to the village after one of their sons took over the farm. I remember my grandparents as a loving couple, who did most things together. They had a beautiful garden with pear trees and grape vines as well as a multitude of different colorful flowers, all of which they tended assiduously.

Once a week they baked their own bread as well as an assortment of delicious cookies, which they would offer to their many visitors. Before going to bed, they always had a cup of coffee upstairs while playing a game or two of Chinese checkers. My grandfather had made the plywood board they used, as well as the different colored marbles for each player, which I think were made of compacted flour and were kept in a cardboard container previously used for orange marmalade made by the Swedish company Findus. All parts of the checkers set, including the marmalade jar, are now with us in Brisbane and still in use by family members and guests. They bring back happy memories of the times I visited my grandparents in the evening and would find them engrossed in their game of checkers.

Every summer my grandparents would organize a family reunion at their house for their eight children and their families. It was always one of the highlights of the summer to play with my nineteen first cousins on my father's side, about half of whom were older than me and half younger. One of our favorite games involved a family member sitting in the middle of the lawn with their eyes closed. This person was "the bear." The others would walk around him in a big circle chanting words beginning: "Bear is sleeping, bear is sleeping in his peaceful den." When the song was finished "the bear" would wake up and the singers would flee, trying their hardest not to be caught by the beast. The person caught would then change places with the bear, or in a variation there would now be two bears to spice up the game.

During those summers I also had contact with relatives on my mother's side, especially her older sisters, who frequently visited us in Viken. Essie, the oldest, was "the wise one," frequently offering us all good advice, but she tended to be rather bossy, and her interference was sometimes resented by my mother. Lalla was "the kind and practical one," who helped us with all manner of domestic chores, including food preparation, as my mother was not interested in housework and we did not always have domestic help during the summers. Lalla often brought her two children on her visits. Hella, who never married, was "the generous one," who always brought all kinds of trinkets and candy for us on every visit, and in this way thoroughly spoiled me as well as my parents. Being an only child, I especially appreciated all the contact with my cousins and aunts, uncles, and grandparents as I was growing up.

During my childhood, another highlight of the summers in Viken was the annual crayfish party at our house for a small select group of family and friends. These parties are a Swedish tradition and are held in August when it is permitted to catch crayfish in Swedish waters. Today I believe most crayfish are frozen and imported from Turkey, but the parties continue to be held in August. The main, sometimes only, food served is crayfish. Traditionally the drinks served with the meal are beer and akvavit, a strong spirit distilled from grain and potatoes, flavored with a variety of herbs. Everyone wears an elaborate paper hat and paper bib, and the dining room is decorated with large orange paper lanterns in the shape of full moons.

One such party which stands out for me occurred in the summer when I was fourteen. The guests were invited for 7 p.m. and that year included Aunt Lalla and her two children (twenty-year-old Gunnar and eighteen-year-old Bodil), Aunt Hella, Agneta and Barbro (my friends from next door), Lave (Lalla's nephew, a handsome bachelor in his late twenties), Walborg (Lalla's best friend from her days working as a hairdresser in Paris), and finally Uncle Evald (Lalla's brother-in-law who was visiting Sweden after having emigrated to Canada in his youth). Cousin Gunnar was always called Gunnar Junior to distinguish him from my father, Gunnar Senior.

Aunt Lalla and her children arrived early by car to help with the dinner preparations. This mainly consisted of boiling potatoes in dill, arranging various types of herring on platters for the first course, and setting the table. They had picked up and brought with them a large number of crayfish, which had been ordered from a fish shop, where they had been cooked and were now ready to eat.

My mother had spent the morning at the hairdresser's and after that, had spent a long time in front of the mirror and in carefully choosing her outfit for the party. Now she appeared with her contribution to the festivities. "I'll do the seating arrangements," she said. "Eva, you and Bodil can sit at the children's table in the room next to the dining room together with Agneta and Barbro. Gunnar Senior can sit between Hella and Lalla. Walborg and Evald can sit at either end of the table, and I will sit between Gunnar Junior and Lave." My mother thus ensured that she would be sitting between two young men with whom she could flirt during the evening.

Once these arrangements were decided, Bodil and I put out the place cards and made sure that each seat had a suitable paper hat. We also put out the paper bibs and napkins, hung up a moon lantern in each room, and put candles on both tables. While all these preparations were going on, my father hid away in the living room and watched the local and international news on TV.

By 8 p.m. the party was in full swing. We were all busy peeling and consuming about a dozen crayfish, lining up the empty shells with attached heads around our plate as proof of having eaten no more than our allotted amount. From the "children's table" we could observe how the adults became increasingly noisy and merry as they sang the well-known traditional Swedish drinking songs that accompanied each sip of the akvavit in front of them. There were different songs depending on whether they swallowed a third, a half, or the whole glass of their drink in one go. Gunnar Junior, who was a student at Lund University and member of the university choir, led the singing wearing a red fez made of paper. Across the table from him, Gunnar Senior wore a real fez brought back from his travels in Turkey. Most of the adults quickly became slightly intoxicated, but there was still an atmosphere of gaiety which was heightened after the sun went down around 9 p.m. and a full moon rose over the house and garden.

After the meal was finished, the guests adjourned to the living room for coffee. I was taking some rubbish out to the bin, when I suddenly came across Lalla crying in the garden in a flustered state. "I've lost my ring," she wailed. "The one Erik gave me before I married Yngve." I spent some time helping her look for it in the grass, but it was never found.

I felt so surprised. Aunt Lalla, who by then had been a widow for quite a few years, was usually very reserved, yet here she was appearing very unlike her usual calm self. In general, Swedes tend to be reserved, but as I recall, it is socially acceptable to drink heavily at a party and let yourself go. The following day you can pretend your behavior, which could have included being overly argumentative, displaying emotional outbursts, or even getting into a physical fight with someone, never happened, or you can blame it on having had one too many. In other words, it is acceptable not to take responsibility for your behavior while under the influence of alcohol, as long as no criminal offence such as drink driving has been committed. Lalla never referred to her outburst or to the ring again.

When my parents bought their house in Viken in 1951, they already had plans to eventually retire in the village. At the same time, they also bought a spare allotment next door to them. I believe they hoped I would marry and bring my family there for summer holidays or perhaps even settle there permanently. Viken was their place in the world and to some extent it is my place too. If I were told to close my eyes and imagine a happy, peaceful place, I would undoubtedly choose Viken, and perhaps more specifically, imagine myself sitting on the beach looking across to Denmark and listening to the sound of the gentle waves. I have more roots in Viken than anywhere else in the world, and it was an admirable effort on my parents' part to try to make me feel at home in Sweden.

However, as it turned out, things did not go according to plan but ended up differently than they had perhaps expected or hoped, in large part due to my father's decision to pursue a diplomatic career.

9. At Home in Washington

My years spent in the United States (New York from 1956 to 1958 and then Washington from 1958 to 1964) coincided with many important historical events. It was the height of the Cold War and a time of considerable flux with the escalation of the Vietnam War. There were protests as well as street riots sparked by Black American racial segregation. The year 1956 saw the re-election for a second term of Eisenhower as President and Nixon as Vice-President. In 1961 John F. Kennedy became President. In the following year he had to deal with the Cuban Missile Crisis. Martin Luther King gave his famous "I have a dream" speech during the March on Washington in 1963. That same year, JFK was assassinated, and Vice-President Lyndon B. Johnson was sworn in as President. On a happier note, Beatlemania had continued to grow in England during 1963, and in 1964 spread to the United States with the arrival of the Beatles for a concert tour. I still have my ticket to the concert at the Washington Coliseum on February 11, 1964.

I remember watching the first televised presidential debate, between Kennedy and Nixon in 1960. The year before we had watched the funeral of John Foster Dulles, Eisenhower's Secretary of State, as it was shown on television. On both occasions my parents told me to be quiet, as "we were watching history in the making." Apart from comments like that, I don't recall my parents giving me their views on any political situations while I was growing up in the States. In fact, I can remember my father actively steering away from discussions on political topics.

I had my tenth birthday in Washington and, before leaving for school, I was allowed to open my presents, which were piled up outside my bedroom. My favorite one was a tape recorder from my parents, and I immediately pretended to be a journalist wanting to interview my father.

"Mr. Ambassador, what's your opinion about nuclear disarmament?" I asked.

My father thought for a moment and then replied, "You have two arms. I have two arms."

I don't think I knew what nuclear disarmament meant but had probably just picked the words up from watching television. However, I understood that my father's answer was a kind of nonsense to avoid answering the question. It stopped me in my tracks and the interview ended abruptly. It was clear that my father did not want to have a serious discussion about the arms race.

Why did we never discuss politics at home within the family? There are several possible explanations and the main one is that when my parents were home and away from the diplomatic life, they wanted to relax and not think about "work." Also, they may have been worried that I would divulge sensitive political views or secret information to people at my school. Finally, my parents may have wanted to protect me from reality as much as possible. We were living in dangerous times in the States during the Cold War, with nuclear attacks by the Russians a distinct possibility. I lived a sheltered life and don't think I even realized the very real threat of nuclear war during the Cuban Missile Crisis with the missiles pointed directly at us in Washington. I don't remember talking about the situation with my parents or feeling the least bit scared. I only remember my piano teacher, Mrs. Abernethy, arriving for my weekly lesson at the most serious point of the crisis, and talking with my father in hushed tones out of my earshot. We then proceeded with my music lesson in the usual manner.

Like Viken, I loved America too, especially the Washington years and the embassy where I grew up. Located at 3900 Nebraska Avenue, its front elevation is wide and impressive in the Spanish Mission style with the main entrance at its center. The house is built in rendered brick and, in my day, it was painted terracotta, but I believe it is now white. In his memoirs from the Washington days, my father describes how the house was bought by the Swedish government in 1950 from the man who had it built in 1925 and first lived in it. This was David Lawrence, later the owner and editor of

The Swedish Ambassador's residence, 3900 Nebraska Avenue, Washington, 1960

the weekly *U.S. News and World Report*. Across the street was a tall television tower belonging to NBC Channel 4, and next door to that a secure naval station. Both are still there today with the naval base currently the U.S. Department of Homeland Security. Near the embassy, just off Ward Circle, is American University. In early 2023 the Swedish government sold the house for 17.3 million dollars.

The diplomatic life had the advantage of providing household staff. As my mother had little interest in housework, this aspect appealed to her. In Washington, there was a cook who had previously worked for the King of Sweden (the grandfather of the present king), a butler/chauffeur, and two maids—all Swedes who lived in the residence. The maids were always recruited from a "domestic training school" in southern Sweden. They would work at the embassy for a year and then be replaced by another couple of trainees.

I haven't been back to the embassy since a visit in my early twenties, but if I close my eyes, I can still clearly see it in front of me from the point of view of an only child with memories of playing, most often by myself, all over the vast house. Immediately inside the entrance there was a long hall with stone tiles on the floor and several tapestries with a medieval motif on the walls. Towards the end of the hall to the right was a winding staircase from which I used to swing down Tarzan-style on a rope, which had been a laundry line. This was probably quite dangerous, but I don't remember my parents being at home to stop me, or anyone of the household staff much noticing what I was up to.

At the end of the hall to the right was a small informal dining room, where we always had breakfast. Immediately opposite the front door was a vast dining room mainly used for official dinners. On the left, the long hall opened onto two very large reception rooms, which I remember as being quite cold all year, probably due to their size. In the first one there was a grand piano which was used for my weekly piano lessons. It was also where we had the annual embassy staff Christmas party, a noisy affair with lots of drinking, singing, and dancing to Swedish Christmas songs. In the second room there was a seven-seater sofa covered in linen with a floral pattern consisting of red, yellow, and blue tulips set against a black background. This was the place where we had the family Christmas on December 24.

Across the hall and slightly to the left of the front door was the library, which we used as the family room. When I came home from school, I would find my mother sitting there watching the soap operas "Days of Our Lives" and "Search for Tomorrow" with our dog Ossian, who had come with us to Washington from Sweden and Larchmont. Later in the day I would do my homework there, often while talking on the phone to one of my school friends and munching on a Finn Crisp banana sandwich, my usual dinner on the many nights my parents were out attending various diplomatic functions. This might seem a meagre fare, but it was enough for me, as my school provided a hot sit-down meal every lunchtime. When my parents were home, we usually had dinner on trays in the family room. This was often the case on Sunday nights when we would watch "Lassie" together, with me hiding under the table, anxiously concerned about Lassie's fate. I would sit at my mother's feet, and she would pat me and scratch my head as though I were a dog. I remember enjoying the physical contact. My mother had many dogs and cats before Ossian and, as she said herself, she felt more confident looking after animals than children. Therefore, it is understandable that I was sometimes treated like her dog.

On the right-hand side of the house extending towards the back, there was a large kitchen wing, which was largely the domain of our Swedish cook, Ida Lindgren. She was very domineering despite being only about 4 feet 6 inches tall. She compensated for this by wearing high Swedish clogs and a peaked chef's cap. I was often chased out from the kitchen area which, together with my mother's lack of kitchen experience, may explain my own lack of interest in food preparation or any kind of cooking.

On the second floor, there was again a long hall. This was where I played dodge ball with our young butler/chauffeur, Pertti, or where I set up my plastic bowling pins and pretended to be in a bowling alley. At the end of the corridor to the right was the official bedroom where members of the Swedish Royal family, Prime Minister Erlander, and other Swedish dignitaries would sleep when visiting Washington. It was also where I would have sleepovers with my friends when we would use the official beds as trampolines, throwing ourselves down from as high as we could with our legs drawn up tight. At the other end of the corridor was my father's room, which was both his bedroom and his study. From there it was possible to make one's way around the inside of the corridor with rooms in this order: two bathrooms, my mother's study with a huge terrace outside it, a small living room with a record player, where my mother would listen to recordings of her favorite musicals such as *South Pacific* and *My Fair Lady*, a bathroom, my mother's bedroom (and Ossian's), another bathroom, and finally my bedroom. Unfortunately, my bedroom was located directly above the official dining room, and I had difficulties going to sleep on many nights, due to the noise and cigarette smoke coming from the floor below. Finally, there was a small linen room where towels, sheets and so on were kept and where the maids taught me how to do the ironing, a task I still enjoy.

In the wing above the kitchen the maids had their rooms, and I also had a "playroom," which was basically a storage space for all the toys I had been given over the years. I didn't play in this room often, but when I did, I usually built a stagecoach using tables and chairs and pretended to be crossing America, no doubt inspired by various television westerns.

Because the house was built on a slope, only part of it had a basement under it. This contained a two-car garage, a large laundry, a table tennis area, and Pertti's rooms. There were two reasons why I avoided the basement. One was unexpectedly stepping on a dead mouse. Another was restricted to the week or so before Christmas each year when the cook would place a large raw fish to soak in a bucket of lye somewhere near the laundry to make "lutefisk." This would give off a terrible smell of rotten fish which often transferred itself to sheets and other laundry hanging up to dry in the basement. "Lutefisk" is part of traditional Swedish Christmas food, which I have never acquired a taste for.

This description of the embassy would not be complete without a mention of the extensive garden: six gently sloping acres at the back of the house leading to a small creek. There were cherry blossom trees to climb and bamboo forests to explore. At the front of the house there were magnolia bushes, crocuses, and baby rabbit burrows. I was often left to my own devices and would play in this wonderful garden by myself. Every year I would have a birthday party for my school friends where the garden would play a central role. I have recently been fortunate enough to reconnect with some of these friends through Zoom meetings and was surprised when quite a few of them remembered these parties.

I was always happy having many different friends, but for a time, I also had a best friend called Anna. It probably seems strange that we often played with our Barbie dolls, even in our early teens. However, the games we played with them were quite sophisticated. At the embassy we usually set up our dolls and their paraphernalia in the small living room where my mother kept her record player. While listening to various records from my mother's collection, we made up elaborate stories involving my dolls, Midge and Jim, and Anna's dolls with the more exciting names Rita and Eddie. Many of our stories had romantic settings. As young teenagers, Anna and I were just imagining what life would be like for us when we were a few years older.

From time to time my mother would walk through the living room and would glance a bit nervously at what was going on in our games. She could probably see that we were not just dressing our dolls for their various activities but putting them into an imagined adult world, which we had yet to experience first-hand. I think Mamma was worried about my growing up and becoming less dependent on her. At this stage in my life, I still did not know much about the facts of life, and my mother seemed happy for me to remain a child under her control. Also, she may have felt jealous of Anna. Mamma still saw herself as my best friend and didn't want any competition from Anna or any other friend.

I was an only child and very much an appendage to the diplomatic life of my parents, probably greatly loved but not consulted about anything important. It might have been better if I'd had a sibling to share the long, lonely stretches of time when my parents were absent. Although I felt very happy during the Washington years, my parents were busier than ever, fulfilling their diplomatic commitments, and I must, to some extent, have resented being left on my own so much. One example of this, which has stayed in my mind, was spending every New Year's Eve alone in front of the television in the family room while my parents were out celebrating with the diplomatic corps, and the household staff were celebrating in some other part of the house without including me.

There were also times when I felt neglected by my mother, even when she was at home and not attending some diplomatic function.

Why, for example, did she watch soap operas every afternoon in Washington when I came home from school instead of asking me about my day or helping me with homework? Why did I feel she often paid more attention to our dog Ossian than to me?

Although my father was often away from home and I saw less of him than of my mother, my memories of him from Washington are positive. On many school nights, he would help me with Latin or French homework before leaving for some diplomatic dinner. If I was upset by something my mother had said to me, I would run to him for comfort, and he always managed to make me feel better.

10. National Cathedral School for Girls (N.C.S.)

A typical school day began at 7:30 when I would sit alone in the family breakfast room poking at a bowl of porridge, which a maid had just placed in front of me. My mother was still in bed after another late night at some diplomatic function. My father had already had his coffee and toast and was upstairs getting ready to be driven to work in downtown Washington. At precisely 7.55 preparatory bugle notes would sound out from the naval station across the street as I gathered my pile of books and notebooks, held together by a large elastic band (no one used a school bag), and waited for our young Swedish chauffeur, Pertti, to bring the car around to the front door to take me to school. The car was an imposing black limousine, which would have a small Swedish flag flying from the bonnet when my father was later driven to his office. I would get into the front seat, holding my books in my lap, and as the reveille proper, augmented through a loudspeaker, started playing at 8, we drove down the circular driveway and turned left into Nebraska Avenue.

    I loved my school in Washington, which I attended from grades 4 to 9. National Cathedral School for Girls (N.C.S.) is an Episcopal school, adjacent to the Washington Cathedral, and the Cathedral was incorporated into many of the school activities. It was, and still is, ranked in the top private schools in the United States. It operated according to an "honor code" whereby we were trusted not to copy another student's work. This code was included in the student handbook and began as follows:

> *We, the students of National Cathedral School, in order to develop further a sense of integrity and of mutual trust have adopted an Honor Code. We consider it a matter of honor that all tests, classwork, and homework be our own.*

At the end of tests and examinations we had to sign the word "Honor," which stood for the pledge: *On my honor I have neither given nor received help on this test.* The system of trust in the students seemed to work well.

At the beginning of the school day, we were again trusted to behave responsibly when we arrived at a huge notice board in the entrance hall and turned over a tag bearing our name to show that we were present. For students in grades 9 to 12, this was the only roll call taken. For lower grades, attendance was taken in the home room. The next step on arrival was to take all the books brought from home for the day to our locker, from which they would be extracted as needed for particular subjects in the breaks between classes. The lockers were in alphabetical order according to surnames, and I was the envy of many of my peers as my locker was next to that of Lucy Johnson, whose father was vice-President and then, after Kennedy's assassination in 1963, President of the United States. She had a handsome, six-foot male bodyguard who was often to be found by her locker when I arrived in the morning. His presence created quite a stir among the school's almost entirely female population.

N.C.S. was an elite, private, all girls' school, attended by day girls and boarders. It had small classes, intelligent, dedicated teachers, and a curriculum well ahead of its time. As I recall, in grade 6, aged eleven, we dissected a cat. I also did a science project which involved studying the regenerative abilities of worms by cutting them in half. In grade 7 we didn't just passively study Shakespeare but were required to assume various roles in *the Merchant of Venice* and *Julius Caesar*, reading the script aloud in as dramatic a manner as we could. We also staged a full performance of *As You Like It*, including a rendition of the songs, for our families and other members of the school community. We were actively involved in the learning process rather than passively absorbing information, and this made us interested in what we were learning and likely to retain the information presented to us.

The Washington Cathedral, a looming Gothic structure, widely regarded as the spiritual home of the nation, was always there in the background. We attended church services in the cathedral every Friday morning. It was there that we were to take refuge in the event of any imminent nuclear attack and where we gathered for prayers after John F. Kennedy's assassination.

To me, the teachers at N.C.S. were revered figures, whom I admired and respected, and many of them have remained role models for me. Some of the teachers I remember best had wonderful names: Millicent (Kent), Gwendolyn (Coney), Geraldine (Wharry), and Ramona (Forbes). I was especially close to Mrs. Forbes, who was my music teacher in years 4 to 8. In addition to the group music lessons at school, she also gave me private voice lessons, and with other pupils I took part in yearly musical performances, which she organized. When she wasn't teaching, Mrs. Forbes was an opera singer and was busy looking after her two children, a boy about my age and a younger daughter. She became a widow at a relatively young age, as her husband was considerably older. Mrs. Forbes and I corresponded for over twenty years after I left Washington. She always wanted me to visit her in the United States, but to my great regret, I never did.

It's also thanks to N.C.S. that I developed a love of English literature. During the school terms, we were required to read and write to satisfy the school curriculum, but starting from grade 4, we were also given a long reading list from which to choose summer vacation reading, followed by written book reports due at the start of each new school year. The lists included classics such as *The Wizard of Oz, Treasure Island*, and *Anne of Green Gables*, but also books such as Helen Keller's biography and *A Night to Remember* about the sinking of the Titanic. This reading was especially important to me, as it was a way to keep me in touch with the English language during the long summer vacations in Viken, where I was surrounded by Swedish relatives and friends and immersed in Swedish language and culture.

11. The Intellectual

As I browse the bookshelves in different rooms of our home in Brisbane, I keep coming across books that once belonged to my mother, all in English, and many of them first editions. There are well-known plays from the 1960s, which she would have read and probably seen on stage during her Washington years, among them: Lillian Hellman, *Toys in the Attic* (1960), Gore Vidal, *The Best Man* (1960), Arthur Miller, *The Misfits* (1961), Dore Schary, *The Devil's Advocate* (1961), and Ronald Millar, *The Affair* (1962). I also find the Australian play, *The Summer of the Seventeenth Doll* (1957) by Ray Lawler, which she might have seen in New York. In addition, we have my mother's copies of famous novels such as: Katherine Anne Porter, *Ship of Fools* (1962), Simone de Beauvoir, *The Mandarins* (1957), Patrick White, *Voss* (1957), Pearl Buck, *Letter from Peking* (1957), Harper Lee, *To Kill a Mockingbird* (1960), Mary McCarthy, *The Group* (1963), and Paul Scott, *The Jewel in the Crown* (1966). Here are also first editions of the English translations of Russian novels such as Boris Pasternak, *Doctor Zhivago* (1958) and Alexander Solzhenitsyn, *The First Circle* (1968) and *August 1914* (1972). I know that my mother also read these novels in Russian during her years in Moscow.

Mamma was clearly a voracious reader who wanted to keep abreast of all the current plays and novels, and to read them in their original language of publication if possible. But, as I was growing up, I had never thought about her as being eager to pursue intellectual interests. Could the early Lund letters throw some light on this side to her character? I was again sitting in front of my computer in the kitchen, reading some more early correspondence from Lund.

Because I was born so late in their lives, I had always seen my parents as old and more like grandparents than parents. Now I was thrilled to have the chance to be privy to their intimate conversations when they were young. Through the letters I could get to know my mother as a person and not just in her role as my mother and as the wife of a diplomat. I could return to the years before I was born and meet my parents when they were young students at Lund University.

My mother wrote:

> Sometimes I wish I could travel out into the world for a while. Alone. You remain quite immature and not used to looking after yourself when you live in the same place your whole life. And you always have to fit in with other people's wishes and commands. (August 1932)

And later:

> I need to get out and see the world a bit (…) I feel quite tired of Lund sometimes. Everyone knows everyone and I can't stand that. (27 September 1935)

I was struck by my mother's longing to escape from Lund and see the world. It reminded me of how my father was always fascinated by Marco Polo's stories about his travels in China and other parts of Asia. While growing up, my father met missionaries through his religious parents, who would talk about their adventures in different parts of the world. He also told me about several uncles who had emigrated from Sweden to America to escape poverty and seek a better life. "When they came home for a visit, it set the imagination in motion. They had so many experiences to share," he said.

Perhaps my parents' interest in languages reflected a mutual longing to escape from the small town of Lund into the wider world. At this early stage of their lives, little did they know that in the future they would spend over thirty years living on four different continents.

Turkish became the focus of my father's linguistic studies at post-graduate level. Thus during 1929 and 1930, he spent six months in East Turkestan, now a province in Northwest China, where he carried out field work for his Ph.D. and where he nearly died of typhoid fever before returning to Lund in April 1930. He was well known in university circles in Lund and went by the nick name "the Turk." Part of his attraction for my mother may have been that he had already traveled to exotic parts of the world. In his memoirs, my father mentioned that when he was suffering from typhoid fever during his research trip, he lost all his hair, which eventually grew back. When he returned to Lund, his *head was covered by short down which was conspicuous and made [him] interesting in the eyes of a certain person.* This is a reference to my mother.

They both took part in the May celebrations at Lund University, which are traditionally held on April 30 and May 1. They fell in love and started a serious relationship at this time.

As I continued to pore over the early letters, I could follow the lives of my parents and add many details to my previous knowledge. Just over a year after they fell in love, my parents became engaged on June 24, 1931, when my mother was twenty-two and my father was twenty-three. Just over a year later they were married. They continued to live in Lund, both working in the University Library, and both pursuing their research interests. My mother studied Russian and Turkish at Lund University and graduated with a B.A. in 1930 and an M.A. in 1934. She wrote her master's thesis on Turkish loan words in Russian, that is, Russian words that have a Turkish origin. My father publicly defended his doctoral thesis and was awarded his Ph.D. on May 31, 1933. During these early years, they were sometimes away from each other while visiting family or friends or while my father was doing research in Copenhagen at the beginning of 1931. He was also away for an extended period during most of 1932 while doing his compulsory military service in Stockholm.

The letters written during their early life together are full of affection and respect for each other. At the outset, my mother admired my father while at the same time feeling intellectually inferior to him. In her first letter to him from July 1930, she stated:

> *It's certainly not bad to receive a letter from an appointed principal librarian. I feel even more ordinary than usual in my capacity as an undergraduate student and temporary dogsbody.*

This must have been a reference to her casual position in the library. In January 1931 she wrote:

> *Things are not going particularly well at the University Library. I have catalogued very few foreign books no matter how hard I try. Help me you who know how!*

While she liked getting help from my father, at the same time, it seemed to upset her that she couldn't be more independent. In February 1931 she said:

> *Of course, I very much like it when you help me. But hate feeling so incredibly inferior. Thus, please forgive my little outburst the other evening.*

Gradually, my mother became more independent and self-confident in her work. In March 1935 she wrote to my father who was on a short visit to Stockholm:

> *I miss you already even though you haven't been away long. But I think it's very good for me to be alone for a while and become a bit more independent and self-sufficient. Agnes Jarring, library assistant with a master's degree, and not just the wife of associate professor Jarring.*

During the second half of 1935, my father traveled to Asia on a six-month research trip funded by a university grant. According to the letters, he was attempting to return to Kashgar in East Turkestan, where he had carried out field work among the Uighurs for his Ph.D. thesis. He had arrived at Srinagar in Kashmir when the Chinese, who were worried about foreign intervention, refused him permission to travel on to Kashgar. There had also been a serious outbreak of the plague in Kashgar, which was another reason for the denial of a visa. Rather than giving up, my father decided to do his research in Srinagar, a hub on the trade routes between Turkestan and India. It was relatively easy for him to find people to interview among the traders, refugees, and pilgrims who used these routes, and he could take extensive notes of their use of various Uighur dialects.

My mother did not accompany my father on this trip due to her full-time job in the University Library and a lack of money. Although she missed him very much, she seemed pleased with her independent life in Lund. In a letter from June 1935, she wrote:

> *My circumstances are in fact really good at the moment. Work which interests me, nice weather, good friends to be together with etc. But my enjoyment is halved when you are not taking part. Also, it's good that I have to manage on my own. When you are home, I always ask you about everything, and don't at all seem to be a modern, emancipated woman.*

The picture of my mother that was beginning to emerge from these letters was very different from the one I previously had of her as a diplomatic wife with no interest in pursuing a career of her own. In the letters I now encountered a modern working woman with a master's degree, a woman who was well-educated, intelligent, and an intellectual.

Lillan and Gunnar as librarians, Lund University, 1936

My mother may not have read aloud to me when I was young or have helped me with homework during the Washington years, but I now recall that from the time I could read, she provided me with books, both in Swedish and later English. It's thanks to her, and not just National Cathedral School, that I developed a love of literature.

I now remember how my mother always encouraged me to study and do research. The result was that I have never doubted my intellectual abilities and I now realize that this is largely due to her positive influence, which I hadn't previously thought about or appreciated. When I received an Australian government scholarship to study at James Cook University in Townsville in 1976, several of my friends in Sweden asked me if I felt worried about the pressures of succeeding in my studies there. This thought had never entered my head. I was more anxious about the long flight to Australia and the dangerous animals I had been warned about on that continent. I had no doubts about my ability to complete the Master of Letters degree.

Without this belief in my intellectual abilities, I would never have overcome the problems I later encountered with my Ph.D. thesis on the Australian author Henry Handel Richardson while I was enrolled at Stockholm University. Despite these difficulties, I never doubted that I would eventually succeed and never thought of giving it all up. Instead, I transferred to Lund University where I completed my degree at the end of 1983 under the excellent supervision of the distinguished Professor Claes Schaar with whom I had previously studied during my undergraduate years. After my arrival in Brisbane, I believed it would be relatively easy to get a tutoring or lecturing position with my Ph.D. in Australian literature. When I could only get casual work in this field, I decided to undertake further study in order to become a teacher, and I eventually got a permanent appointment at the University of Queensland.

In retrospect, I realize that to a great extent it was my mother's encouragement that provided me with the intellectual self-confidence I needed to do well in my university studies.

12. Going Native

An integral part of diplomatic life is the constant moving from country to country with an inevitable sense of dislocation. Many, perhaps even most, diplomatic children live in various countries/cultures, only staying for two to three years in each place and then having to move on in step with their parents' postings. Many of them may have little contact with their own country or with their relatives back home. In later life these children may react in different ways.

Among my friends who grew up as children of Swedish diplomats, one, who had limited contact with her own country as a child, always longed to get married and settle down in Sweden with a house in Stockholm and a summer place in the countryside. In fact, she managed to achieve this goal. Two of my other Swedish friends, also from a diplomatic background, reacted in the opposite way. Instead of longing for a life in Sweden, they left their native country soon after high school and married foreigners. One settled in New Zealand and one in Australia. Both hardly ever visit Sweden and have to a great extent forgotten their native tongue.

Many less fortunate diplomatic children are unable to feel they fully belong anywhere in the world. They feel they have no home in any particular country or even in their own country. This is because they have changed their residence so often during their childhood and have not kept in touch with their native country. I have heard stories of mental health issues, drug and alcohol abuse, and even suicide.

Most diplomats tend to be transferred after just a few years. This might be for them to gain experience in a variety of countries, or it might be a way to ensure that they remain objective in their diplomatic reporting and don't identify overly much with the country of their current posting, colloquially termed "going native." During the Cold War, the top two diplomatic postings in the Swedish Department of Foreign Affairs were Ambassador to the United States and Ambassador to the Soviet Union. The people who held these positions did so for a long period of time, unlike the short-term postings in other countries. Thus, my father was appointed Ambassador to the U.S.A. from 1958 to '64 and Ambassador to the U.S.S.R. from 1964 to'73. Before him, Erik Boheman had been Sweden's Ambassador in Washington from 1948 to '58 and Rolf Sohlman was Sweden's Ambassador in Moscow for seventeen years, with ten of those years as dean of the diplomatic corps.

My own experience is therefore different to that of many other diplomatic children. While I was growing up, from the age of seven to fifteen, I spent six years in Washington and before then two years outside New York when my father was Ambassador to the United Nations. Because I'd spent so many years in the United States and had continuous contact with Sweden through my summers in Viken, instead of feeling that I didn't fully belong anywhere, my problem was fully identifying with two separate countries/cultures— an American one as well as a Swedish one.

———

I was seven and a half when I arrived in America. At that time, I could speak Swedish fluently and was beginning to read and write it as well. However, I did not know a word of English. I had only spent one month in grade 1 at a school in Stockholm, but because Americans start school at the age of six, I was placed in grade 2 in Chatsworth Avenue School in Larchmont. This was a large, state-run school. I can still vividly remember my first day there. Perhaps to make me feel more secure and supported, the teacher, Miss Najim, put my little desk next to hers at the front of the classroom with my desk facing the class, so that around twenty pairs of eyes stared at me with curiosity. Then there was a strange language all around me, which I could not understand. I had to stay in this position within the classroom for many days, just listening and observing without actively taking part in the other children's activities. This passive absorption of the English language continued at home where I spent hours each day in front of the television, which was a new phenomenon for me not yet encountered in Sweden. With my father being away at the U.N. all day, and my mother busy entertaining or being entertained on the diplomatic circuit, I was free to watch whatever appeared on the screen. There were a lot of cartoons, Shirley Temple movies, and westerns.

Gradually, through this immersion, I began to understand more and more English and finally, after a few months, even to speak and read it. By the end of the second quarter of grade 2 (probably around February), my report card states: *Eva has made great gains. Her grasp of the English language is good!* For the first quarter of grade 3, I was given a "good" in English, but my reading and spelling were "not up to grade level." However, by the end of the school year, I received "excellent" in all three report card categories.

I can still recall some of my early problems with learning English. At Easter we were all in our Easter bonnets singing about the Easter parade on Fifth Avenue in New York, according to the famous song by Irving Berlin. It seems like yesterday when I got confused about a word in the lyrics. I felt sure that it was the "thermometers" and not the *photographers* that would *snap us* (take our photos). It may be that some of the other children laughed at my mistake because I remember it so vividly. I also had problems with pronouncing "th," which is a sound not found in Swedish. I especially recall trying to say "thumb" correctly, probably because I had finally managed to stop sucking my thumb at the very late age of seven. In those days it was common for pupils to have an I.Q. test and I was given one, I think in grade 3. One of the questions was, "Where does the sun set?" My answer was, "The sky." I felt very upset because I did not properly understand the questions or how to answer them. I received a very low I.Q. score, which I could luckily rectify a year or two later in Washington.

When I attended the prestigious National Cathedral School for Girls (N.C.S.), I soon discovered that the academic demands in this private school were considerably higher than they had been in the state-run school in Larchmont. For the first quarter in year 4, I only received a grade of "fair" in English. Moreover, during my whole first year at N.C.S., I had to attend "special English" classes in addition to mainstream English. I had completely forgotten about these extra classes until I found my old report cards. I have no recollection of what I was taught in these classes, or whether I was alone or taught with other students who were also from a non-English-speaking background.

From my report cards I can trace how over the years at N.C.S., my English steadily improved. By the end of year 5, I achieved an "A-" in the three report card categories English, Reading, and Writing, together with the comment: *Eva's work in English skills has achieved the quality of excellence.* My final report card for year 7 reads: *Her command of English is excellent: in fact, it is far better than that of some of her classmates for whom it is a native language!*

Apart from a few initial problems acquiring English, I felt at home in the United States from the start and was quickly pledging allegiance to the American flag hanging at the front of my year 2 classroom in Larchmont. Every morning we would listen to the headmaster's cheerful greeting over the loudspeaker, "Good morning, boys and girls," after which we would turn towards the flag and together recite:

> *I pledge allegiance to the flag of the United States of America and to the republic for which it stands, one nation under God, indivisible, with liberty and justice for all.*

I also enthusiastically took part in fall-out drills, hiding under the desk along with my fellow pupils. This was a common practice during the Cold War years with the ever-present threat of a nuclear attack.

Although my English was gradually improving and I was becoming increasingly American, the Swedish part of me had still been stronger during the two Larchmont years when I was seven to nine years old.

As the Ambassador's residence, the house and garden in Washington were officially on Swedish soil and thus part of Sweden, but for me they were very much part of my emerging American self. Except for the relatively infrequent and short periods of time when I was with my parents or the Swedish household staff, I was alone, playing by myself in various parts of the house and garden, and often watching American TV programs in the family room. I'm confident that I was thinking in English, as this was quickly becoming the stronger language for me. If I was not alone, I was with various American friends who had been invited over to play or for a sleepover.

I have always regarded myself as bilingual, that is, completely fluent in both Swedish and English, starting from the years I spent growing up in Washington. From this time, I also began to have a sort of dual personality with two countries which I called home. At school, I was completely American. At home, I switched to being Swedish, speaking only Swedish to my parents and our Swedish

My American self, Washington, 1958

domestic staff. Many diplomatic children tend to mix languages. I never did. If I had an American school friend over for a meal, I would speak English to her, Swedish to my parents, and then translate the Swedish back to English for the benefit of my friend. It was a way of keeping my two personalities intact.

I feel sure that by the time I attended grade 4 in Washington, none of my school friends would have seen me as foreign. They never made me feel like an outsider and I always felt confident in my American self. However, I remember that on the summer holidays in Viken, I was sometimes teased by the local children because they thought I spoke Swedish with an American accent. It felt hurtful to be seen as not truly belonging to my own country and not being able to fully master my own first language. Already at around the age of nine or ten, my English-speaking, American self was becoming stronger than my Swedish self.

How would I describe my two personae during the Washington years? My Swedish self would always strive to please my mother, to be the "good little girl" she had always wanted, who always obeyed her and was kind to her. My American self was more adventurous and beginning to rebel against the control my mother had over my Swedish self. I remember my mother commenting that she thought the American way of life had influenced me negatively in that it made me more independent and rebellious.

The way I used my two languages also had an impact on the development of my two personae and made my American self quickly become the stronger of the two. I only used Swedish for speaking and listening when at home, and only rarely used it for writing infrequent short letters to my relatives in Sweden and for reading their replies. On the other hand, my use of English, especially through school lessons and homework, involved many more hours each day than my use of Swedish and was much broader and more creative, employing all four language skills.

I now wonder whether my parents were aware that they had a budding American living in their home. I also wonder whether my mother was fully aware of the developing change in me; that I was growing away from her, and that this was the inevitable result of being the child of a diplomat living in a foreign country.

13. Abandoned

For a time, I had found a perfect balance between my two selves: my Swedish self during the long summer vacations in Sweden, and my American self in Washington. For me this balance was essential for my normal, happy existence, and I believed it would continue for the foreseeable future.

Then one day, towards the end of 1963 when I was fourteen, something happened which was to change my life forever. My father asked me to come into his study after I had finished my homework because he wanted to talk to me. On entering his study, I noticed that he was ill-at-ease and didn't know how to start the conversation, which was unusual for him.

Taking a deep breath, he said, "You know how the diplomatic life is very exciting and involves living in many interesting places in different parts of the world. Well, we've had almost eight wonderful years here in the United States, but it's now time for us to move on. I've been appointed Sweden's Ambassador to the Soviet Union. We leave for Moscow in January."

At first, I found it hard to digest the full significance of what he was saying. "But this is my home. I love it here and all my friends are here. I can't leave!"

"Mamma and I have discussed this, and we'll both have to leave in January, but you wouldn't have to leave straight away. You'll be able to finish grade 9 at N.C.S. as a boarder until the end of the school year in June."

"Why can't Mamma stay here with me? Why can't I stay on in my room at the embassy? Or why can't I stay with my friend, Anna, and her family? I could offer to clean their house for them. I would do anything rather than go to boarding school ... Can I come back to Washington to continue in grade 10 even if you're in Moscow?"

By this stage, I was in tears. My father did his best to placate me. He had to use his best diplomatic skills to explain the situation and persuade me that the best plan was for me to board at N.C.S. for a few months.

My world really started to fall apart when I realized that I would not be returning to the States after June, and moreover, I was told that since there were no suitable schools in Moscow, I would become a boarder at Sigtuna Humanistiska Laroverk in Sweden from the following September. This was a private school near Stockholm attended largely by the children of diplomats, the aristocracy and, at that time, by the future King of Sweden, Carl Gustav. Not only was I losing one of "my countries," and the strongest part of my identity, but I was also losing my family. I was fourteen years old and, except for visits during school holidays, I was never going to live at home with my parents again.

Looking back at the conversation with my father, I wonder why my parents hadn't better prepared me for the move from Washington. According to my father's memoirs, the Swedish government had informed him already in September 1963 that he would become Ambassador to the Soviet Union early in the new year. However, as I recall, I was blissfully unaware of the change awaiting me until just before Christmas. Also, I don't remember any conversations with my parents where we discussed the fact that diplomats are constantly moved from place to place. I don't recall ever worrying about having to leave Washington.

My parents knew how much I loved America and must have realized how upset I would be by the move. Maybe they wanted me to be happy in my ignorance for as long as possible. Or maybe they told me earlier and I had decided to block it out of my mind. In any case, in retrospect, I felt ill-prepared for the news of the move, and it came as a shock to me.

In his memoirs, my father has written the following paragraph about my plight:

> *Fourteen-year-old Eva was to stay on alone in Washington to continue her American schooling. It was impossible to change to a Swedish school in the middle of a school year. (…) It was not a happy Eva that we parted from. In those days it was one of the disadvantages of the diplomatic life: to be forced to leave a post without any consideration being taken of what the parents and a lonely fourteen-year-old girl-child thought and felt. I remember that on my return to Stockholm, I raised the issue with the relevant authority. I thought it was cruel and wasn't contradicted.*

From my point of view, it was more than "cruel." It was a disaster. As an immature only child, I was going to be separated from my parents, to whom I was overly tied. Also, I did not want to give up my American identity and live in "Sick Tuna," my derogatory English name for Sigtuna. I knew that Moscow was far away in Eastern Europe behind the "Iron Curtain" and in the heart of "enemy territory." I clearly saw the move to Moscow as a threat. In one of my drawings from this time, I have depicted the beautiful embassy and garden in Washington, but in the foreground are two gigantic wooden Russian dolls with a menacing look in their eyes. They are hugely out of proportion in relation to the house, which looks about to be swallowed up by them.

I have no memory of saying goodbye to my parents, only of our chauffeur, Pertti, dropping me off with my bags at the boarding house at N.C.S. I have probably suppressed those memories as being too painful.

Leaving home at this point completely changed my life and my relationship with Mamma. Up to then, I had been very close to my mother (although we had our arguments) but afterwards I kept myself at a distance from her. During the five months I was by myself in the States, I tried to break free from my parents, in particular my mother, by writing the slogan "independence above all" at the top of every entry in my diary. I believed that if I could be independent, I wouldn't be hurt again. At the time, I didn't know how my mother experienced our forced separation. Was it all a disaster for her too?

I don't remember feeling unhappy after my parents left. I still did well at school, although a poem I wrote during this time had my teachers asking me if I was sad and missing my parents. It ran:

The sea air was eerie
I stood on the deck
And studied the night sea
All drenched in darkness
A wind of disaster
Swept over the sea
I heard the sea murmur
That it wanted me
I threw off my blanket
I jumped in the sea
I was met by the waves
That devoured me
The sea air's still eerie
Though not on the deck
I still see the night sea
All drenched in blackness

I am certain that I didn't have any thoughts of committing suicide when I wrote the poem. Instead, I can trace its inspiration to some poems we had recently been studying in my English class: Longfellow's well-known poem *The Wreck of the Hesperus* and Alfred Noyes' perhaps less well-known *The Highwayman* with the repetition of its first lines at the end of the poem. For my poem I was also drawing on the Atlantic crossings that I had made with my mother. While she would be having her usual cocktail before dinner in the first-class lounge, I would stand at one of the wide windows and look down on the huge swells many feet below, mesmerized by the rhythm of the waves breaking against the ship.

During those boarding school months at N.C.S., I cannot recall feeling unhappy on the inside and trying to hide this from the people around me. I do, however, remember a few occasions when I felt sad and lonely. One was on my fifteenth birthday at the end of April. The day fell on a weekend and many of the boarders had been given day passes to go into the city center or weekend passes to visit family or friends. I was one of the few boarders left in the school and no one knew that it was my birthday. This was in stark contrast to the way I had celebrated in the past during my years in America, with many presents from my parents and the Swedish household staff, and birthday parties with lots of games and delicious food. One of our Swedish maids, with whom I have kept in touch, once sent me an extract from her diary with a description of my ninth birthday in 1958 in Larchmont, which is typical of my birthdays in the States and shows just how spoilt I was! Here is a summary of her extract:

> *Eva's parents gave her a swing, a bicycle, some clothes, and a big globe. The household staff gave her a bracelet and a necklace. At noon ten classmates arrived for lunch. The menu was Swedish meatballs, mashed potatoes, and ice-cream. After lunch they had a ride on a (rented) pony for an hour. At 3 p.m. new guests arrived and were given coca cola and ice-cream. In the evening there was a birthday*

dinner for the family and staff when all the adults drank champagne.

Another unhappy occasion during boarding school in Washington was when I contracted German measles (rubella) and had to spend two weeks in isolation in a far-off corner of the boarding house. My only visitor during this period was the very masculine-looking resident nurse with the implausible name, Miss Tarbox. She would appear from time to time to ask me in her booming voice how I was feeling, before leaving me alone again. My parents later told me how worried they were during this time as they hadn't received my usual weekly letter. I must have felt too ill to write and no one had thought to inform them that I was in the infirmary.

It was difficult to adjust to my new living arrangements as a boarder, especially during the first few weeks. I had been used to having a large room of my own in the embassy, whereas now I had to share a tiny room with two other girls who were in the year below me and with whom I had had no previous contact. As my parents were often attending diplomatic functions in the evenings, I was accustomed to putting myself to bed at around 10 or sometimes later after doing homework, reading, or watching television. As a boarder, I was now subjected to a strict "lights out" regime, which as I recall was on the dot of 9 p.m. On one occasion I was in the process of changing the hem of a skirt, which was too long, and had pins all over my bed when Mrs. Hunter, our house mistress, came around and turned the lights off, leaving me to cope as best I could in the dark. As a boarder, I also got into the habit of setting an alarm for 6 a.m. so that I could spend my customary amount of time doing homework before the rising bell at 6:45.

It was hard visiting the embassy, which had been my home for many years. The new ambassador had a daughter my age and I was invited to the residence once or twice. It was horrible to see "my" room occupied by this stranger and the changes that had been made to "my" home. Also, the maids and chauffeur, who were young people in their twenties and whom I had seen as my friends, were now busy looking after a new family. Pertti had always been especially friendly towards me, often buying me candy at a "nickel-and-dime" store after picking me up from school and playing dodgeball or table tennis with me when we got home if he was free. Now I felt excluded and alone as an "outsider."

14. "Sick Tuna"

I remember feeling distinctly ill-at-ease on my first day at the Swedish co-educational boarding school in Sigtuna, a small town on the outskirts of Stockholm. It was September 1964 and all the students, accompanied by their parents, were gathered on a vast outdoor terrace high up on a hill overlooking Lake Malaren. This terrace was surrounded on three sides by neoclassical buildings, leaving the fourth side open to the beautiful view. The most imposing building was in the middle and was built to resemble a Greek temple. I later discovered it was one of the boys' dormitories, while the other two buildings housed classrooms. As had been the case at N.C.S., there was no requirement to wear uniforms, and students, as well as their parents, were dressed according to the latest fashion.

The junior school at Sigtuna consisted of years 1 to 5 with students in year 1 aged ten or eleven. The senior school comprised three further years. Students could enter the school at any level, but many of them had commenced in year 1 of the junior school. I was fifteen when I arrived and was entering year 5 of the junior school. Most of the students in my class already knew each other from previous years and had formed friendship groups that excluded me. In addition, many were from the Swedish aristocracy, and I could tell by the way they gathered in small groups, chatting amongst themselves while ignoring everyone else, that they were unlikely to let someone like me, who was not from an aristocratic background, join their group. This kind of arrogance based on class distinctions was quite unlike the democratic atmosphere of N.C.S., where any distinctions in the school were merit-based.

Although I had managed to become a bit more independent during my time alone in Washington, I nevertheless felt extremely anxious and sad when my mother left me on my first day at Sigtuna. These feelings quickly passed as I became involved in life at the school.

After the high academic standards at N.C.S., the academic standards at Sigtuna were a disappointment to me. My first year was spent doing the equivalent of O-Levels with a mixture of science and arts subjects. For the following three senior school years, we had to choose one of three "lines" or "streams" of study: the "classical" line with the emphasis on Latin and languages; the mathematical line; or the less rigorous line of social sciences. I chose the classical line and successfully completed my final year in the following subjects: English, Swedish, French, Latin, and History (as majors) with Religion, Philosophy, Social Science, Music, and Physical Education (as minors).

After the outstanding teachers at N.C.S., I was disappointed by a few of the teachers in Sigtuna whose teaching methods seemed to be old-fashioned in comparison. Their idea of a good lesson was to read from a textbook and then talk at us for most of the lesson, rather than letting us be active and do the talking. However I had a wonderful Latin teacher, Miss Tegner, who had the hairstyle of a Roman matron and who would spend her holidays taking trips to Italy like Muriel Spark's Miss Jean Brodie. She would bring back lots of slides to show us on her return. There was also my French teacher, Mr. Viotti, whose name in Swedish sounds like "we eighty," which he in turn jokingly translated into French as "Monsieur Nous quatre-vingts." This was also the name we knew him by. He would often entertain us by doing Maurice Chevalier song and dance routines when the lessons needed livening up.

I spent four years in Sigtuna, and apart from improving my Swedish (especially my reading and writing skills which were limited before this time), memorizing some facts about Swedish history and literature, and struggling to learn O-Level German in one year, I don't recall learning a great deal more than what I already knew from my time at N.C.S. When I arrived at Sigtuna, I was years ahead in Mathematics, Latin, French, and of course English. I was naturally not alone in this experience, as many of my peers in Sigtuna had also attended excellent schools abroad and were bilingual or in some cases even trilingual.

While this lack of learning opportunities was a disadvantage, it also proved to be an advantage for me. Having left the United States forever in June 1964, I had to find some new means of keeping the American part of my identity intact. Because I didn't need to study long hours to pass, I had plenty of time to cultivate my "American" or English-speaking self. My main way of doing this was through my friendship with a girl called Asa, whose father was at the time Sweden's Ambassador to Thailand.

We were two of the small number of new students in our year and soon became close friends. We also discovered that we both did not get on well with our respective roommates. When we asked if we could share a room, our housemother agreed, and we were allocated one with no door but just a curtain separating it from the hall. We were both fluent in English, so to ensure that our conversations were private, we started our lifelong habit of conversing with each other in English rather than Swedish. (We were lucky because the students in the surrounding rooms were not among those who had grown up in an English-speaking environment before attending Sigtuna.)

Our English was much better than that of our teachers, and soon we were no longer required to attend English classes, but only had to sit for various essay-writing exams where we had to write a certain number of words on a previously unseen topic. Before each exam, we would decide on one or two unusual words which we would incorporate into our essays to confound our teacher.

The day before one exam, I found Asa in our room feeding her exotic Thai fish, which was kept in a large glass bowl. "I thought of a word we could use tomorrow. How about *valetudinarian*," she suggested. "It has lots of syllables. It's a noun meaning *a person in poor health*."

I also liked the sound of this multi-syllabic word and quickly agreed. "What about *peccary* for a second word," I proposed. "It means *a medium-sized, pig-like mammal found in Central and South America*. It looks like the word *pessary*, a contraceptive device."

We wanted to shock our teacher who probably wouldn't have known the meaning of peccary, but would no doubt have known the similar-looking term. My opening line in the exam was: "I could tell by his walk that he was a valetudinarian." My story was about a suicidal immigrant to Sweden who was given the advice to buy a peccary to cheer himself up.

We always got As on our essays, but there were never any comments concerning our often quite eccentric and baffling plots. Although I didn't learn much academically in Sigtuna, I was nevertheless happy there, as I could, to some extent, keep my American and Swedish identities in balance through my friendship with Asa.

A few years ago, I was rereading the novel *The Group* by the American writer Mary McCarthy. It describes the lives of eight young women, including their sexual relationships, after they graduate from Vassar College in 1933. Imagine my surprise when I found the following passage, which occurs after one of the women, Dottie, has embarked on an affair with a divorced artist named Dick:

> *"Get yourself a pessary." Dick's muttered envoi, as he propelled her firmly to the door the next morning, fell on*

Dottie's ears with the effect of a stunning blow. Bewildered, she understood him to be saying "get yourself a peccary," and a vision of a coarse piglike animal they had studied in Zoology passed across her dazed consciousness, like a slide on a screen … (p. 47)

This passage must have been the source for the word "peccary" which Asa and I decided to use in our exam, but I have no recollection of having read *The Group* at this time. The novel is among the books which I inherited from my mother, and it's likely that I read it during one of my Christmas vacation visits to Moscow from Sigtuna. Previously I had always thought I had chosen the word "peccary" from a book called *Classification of the Animal Kingdom*, which Asa, who loved animals, had given me. This book even had a picture of a peccary.

I would have been fascinated by the detailed descriptions of sexual relations to be found in *The Group*, as at this stage my knowledge of such matters was negligible. When I was around ten, one of our maids in Washington had tried to tell me about the "facts of life" by not very clearly describing the life of the animals on the farm where she grew up in Sweden. The vague knowledge I thus gleaned was not greatly augmented by the book about adolescent bodies and behavior, which my mother left in my room when I would have been about thirteen or fourteen. She left it on my bed without making any comment and never mentioned it again.

Later, among the material in my study in Brisbane, I recently found one of the first essays I wrote for my Swedish teacher, which shows my positive opinion of Sigtuna for other reasons than giving me time to devote to my English-speaking self. The essay topic was "What it is like to attend a boarding school" and the date was November 23, 1964. Here is my English translation of some extracts:

(…) It's actually quite fun to live in a boarding school. You make wonderful friends, both girls and boys. They are not

ordinary young people, but instead those who have lived in other parts of the world. They can tell you stories about what it's like there in a way that makes you feel as though you have been there yourself.

When you live in a boarding school, you feel like you have lots and lots of siblings. In reality I don't have any and that's precisely why I am so happy to have so many here.

You also learn a lot about how to conduct yourself, both towards adults and your peers. For example, you try to overcome your faults. I know I have already changed a lot since arriving here.

Many people think that boarding schools are too strict, but I don't agree. Because I am an only child, my parents are overly protective. They hardly ever allow me to go out. (…) Here you are just one of several hundred and no one has time to spoil you.

I must have felt lonely growing up without siblings. In addition, the extracts imply that while I was living at home, I wasn't taught to consider the feelings of others and had certain negative personality traits, which I needed to overcome. My mother often commented on my stubbornness and, as an only child, I was no doubt self-centered and spoilt as well.

These extracts also demonstrate how I welcomed my increasing independence from my parents. Before Sigtuna, I had very little contact with boys. The above comment about my parents not letting me go out no doubt refers to the summer of 1964 in Viken when I was fifteen. There were many young people my age in the village who would meet at informal parties at someone's house, but my parents still treated me like a child, and I was not allowed to attend. Because Sigtuna was a coeducational school, I was suddenly meeting boys on a daily basis and attending school dances on many

Saturday nights. I can still remember the first dance I went to and the shock I felt when I observed couples dancing close together and even kissing each other on the dance floor. Before Sigtuna I was very innocent and had never been kissed.

Although I seemed to feel happy to be separating from my parents and becoming a young independent woman, the last part of my essay shows that it was still a struggle:

> *On the other hand, there are of course disadvantages with attending a boarding school. For example, you so seldom see your parents. In a way you need your parents more than ever precisely in those years when you are growing up.*

15. Moscow Interludes

In our house in Brisbane, we have many Russian paintings belonging to my parents which they acquired during their years at the embassy in Moscow. Most of these are by the Russian nonconformist artist, Anatoly Zverev. Three of them are large paintings measuring 84 cm by 60 cm depicting the head and shoulders of my mother. Two of these are studies for the final portrait which the embassy staff presented to my father on his sixtieth birthday. Every day I walk past this portrait hanging on the living room wall and it reminds me of my visits to Moscow over many years.

I spent nine Christmases in Moscow while my father was Sweden's Ambassador to the Soviet Union from 1964 to 1973 at the height of the Cold War. Sometimes I would visit Moscow during Easter breaks as well, because it was only a two-hour flight from Stockholm or Copenhagen. In Moscow, the Swedish Ambassador's residence was a spacious building in the city center, within easy walking distance of Red Square. Known as Mindovsky House, after the millionaire owner who commissioned it prior to the 1917 Revolution, it is one of the finest examples of Art Nouveau architecture in Moscow. It is located at 44 Ulitsa Vorovskogo (Vorovski Street) and was built in 1903.

The house had a strange layout. There was a large entrance hall, at the back of which was a door. This door was usually kept closed and it led to four large bedrooms. The hall was dominated by an imposing marble staircase leading to the floor above. At the top to separate from her and become independent after Washington, I still wanted her love, not presents.

I especially recall an occasion when I arrived in Moscow for Christmas holidays from boarding school in Sweden. In my room my mother had laid out the usual invitation cards to various Christmas parties, together with letters for me that had already arrived in the diplomatic pouch transported to us by courier from the Department of Foreign Affairs in Stockholm once a week. (This was the way we received mail at the embassy in Moscow in those days, as the ordinary mail was slow and likely to be read by the KGB.) In addition, my mother had displayed various presents for me around the room. I recognized that these were bought in one of the special stores for foreigners where Russians were not allowed to shop. There was an amber necklace and a Russian lacquer box decorated with animals, both of which are still with me in Brisbane. There was also a fur cap with ear flaps. Of course, it was kind of my mother to give me presents in addition to the ones I would receive from her at Christmas a week later, but this kindness was negated when I was left alone just hours after my arrival. On the plane I had looked forward to spending a nice evening with my mother, but after quickly greeting me, she returned to reading her current book without any further interaction with me. In this case, my mother wasn't pulled away from me by diplomatic commitments. The presents couldn't make up for the fact that I felt rejected by my mother. I felt upset and ran to my father who comforted me.

Although I did not always get along with my mother during my visits to Moscow, my breaks there were a wonderful time when I could cultivate my two personae. I could speak Swedish at home in the embassy with my parents and Swedish maids, and when I met the other Swedish diplomats and their children. At the same time, I could be my English-speaking self at the many Christmas parties arranged for the diplomatic teenagers and young adults from all over the world, who were visiting their parents from boarding schools and universities in their own country. (It was unusual for any of them to study in Moscow, as there were no international schools and studying at a local school meant doing so in Russian, which is not an easy language to learn.) In the group of young people there were, among others, Belgians, Americans, Germans, Austrians, and quite a few South Americans. Our lingua franca was always English.

During the Christmas vacation of 1968, the Beatles' song "Back in the U.S.S.R." had just been released. We young people played this song over and over again at every social occasion, as we could identify with many of the lines in the song, starting from the first one: *Flew in from Miami Beach B.O.A.C.* We had all just flown in (from various countries), some of us perhaps even on a plane operated by the British Overseas Airways Corporation. Then there was: *Been away so long I hardly knew the place / Gee, it's good to be back home.* We felt bonded by the words. We all felt we were back home, which at that time for us was the U.S.S.R. If I were to run into any of my friends from those Moscow days, I'm sure they would also remember the significance of those lyrics. During our holidays in Moscow, we lived an elitist, sheltered existence, but at the time most of us were probably unaware of this, or at least didn't think much about it.

One of the highlights of Christmas vacations in Moscow was the New Year's Eve ball held every year at the Canadian Embassy by the dean of the diplomatic corps, Ambassador Robert Ford. The ball was usually a masquerade and guests would often hire elaborate costumes from the Bolshoi theater. Guests would include senior diplomats and their wives from most of the embassies in Moscow, together with their children if aged fifteen or over. Ambassador Ford and his vivacious Brazilian wife Teresa would receive their guests at the top of a marble staircase leading into a vast ballroom. For me it was a most welcome change from the lonely New Year's Eves I had spent by myself at home in Washington while my parents were out celebrating with other members of the diplomatic corps.

16. Literature and Curries

After graduating from Sigtuna, I wanted to return to the United States and attend university there. However, this was well beyond my parents' financial means. Also, they must have realized how much I missed my life in America, but no doubt wanted their only child to settle in Sweden and thus stay closer to them. Moreover, they were keen for me to attend their old university in Lund, and suggested I study Russian as I had already picked up some of the language through visiting them in Moscow during many vacations.

Just as England has two ancient universities, Oxford and Cambridge, Sweden has two old universities, Uppsala and Lund. Located in a small town in southern Sweden, Lund University was founded in 1666. Today it has about 40,000 students in a town with a population of 100,000. The town is dominated by a magnificent Romanesque cathedral founded in the eleventh century.

I spent over four years in Lund, from September 1968 to early 1973. It was the time of demonstrations against the Vietnam War and apartheid in South Africa. In contrast to the conservative students I had mixed with at N.C.S., Sigtuna, and during vacations in Moscow, the students I met at Lund were mostly left-wing. In the past I had always been admired for living in an embassy, but now I came in for a lot of criticism. "How could I visit my parents in Moscow and live in luxury in an embassy at the expense of the Swedish taxpayers?" I must admit I hadn't seen it this way before.

In fact, when I began my studies in Lund, I had very little

socio-political knowledge or awareness of the world. One embarrassing example of this occurred early on. During my first years in Lund, I stayed at the International Students' House, which had been inaugurated in 1959 by the then U.N. Secretary-General Dag Hammarskjold, who was from Sweden. The house was meant to foster international understanding by bringing together Swedish students and overseas students from all over the world. In the corridor in which I was living, my room was the first one on the left as you came up the stairs to the second floor. There were twelve rooms in my corridor, including mine, and the occupants of the other eleven rooms all had to pass my room to get to theirs. Having just returned to Lund after spending the Christmas of 1968 partying with my diplomatic friends in Moscow, I had many happy memories of the city and decided to decorate the outside of my door with postcards of Red Square, Gorky Park, and the Moscow River by night. It didn't take long before there was a pounding on my door, punctuated by screams and sobbing. When I came out, Vera from down the corridor had ripped the postcards off the door and was stamping on them. She was from Czechoslovakia, and in August 1968 her country had been invaded by the Soviet Union to suppress the liberal reforms introduced by Dubček. I knew where Vera was from and I knew about the recent invasion, but I hadn't realized that displaying postcards from the Soviet Union on my door might be interpreted by her as my being sympathetic to the Soviet cause. I had been highly insensitive.

I was not very happy during my first few semesters in Lund, and I realize now that this was largely because I had lost contact with my English-speaking persona. In the beginning I didn't mix with the foreign students at International House. Instead, the students I met were typically Swedish with no wide experience of the world.

I remember being especially annoyed by the so-called "men," who were living in various student dormitories but who would return home on weekends so that their mothers could help them do their laundry. However, after a year or so things improved. Asa, who had been traveling abroad, arrived in Lund to study medicine and we could continue our conversations in English which we had started in Sigtuna. What is more, I finished the Russian part of my arts degree and continued by studying English (both the language and literature), which I loved from the start and which I had not seriously studied since the inspiring lessons at N.C.S.

At this time, I also met the man who was to become my first serious boyfriend. I had, of course, had relationships with boys before, but they had been platonic, at least on my part, as I was late to develop physically and hadn't been ready for a sexual relationship. For a few years at boarding school in Sigtuna I had a purely platonic relationship with Mr. M., the nickname Asa and I conferred on him, which I will use here. The relationship suited us both as he made no attempt to do more than kiss me and hold my hand, and we both valued our strong friendship.

Now in Lund I had fallen in love with a handsome Indian from South Africa named Jaya. He was two years older than me and also lived in International House. He walked very quietly in suede shoes and often wore a tan suede jacket. His attire and elegant movements reminded me of a graceful gazelle. When he first kissed me, I kept my eyes open so that I wouldn't lose sight of his handsome face. I couldn't believe that someone with his good looks could be attracted by me. I seriously fell in love and for the first time could identify with what poets and other writers had described as their experiences of being in love. (Many years later, giving birth to my daughters gave me similar feelings of being part of humanity and sharing a universal experience.)

In retrospect, one of Jaya's main attractions for me was no doubt the fact that he spoke perfect English. He had studied in London before coming to Lund and knew a lot about English literature. His favorite novel was *Sons and Lovers* by D.H. Lawrence. He told me how he identified with the main character, Paul Morel, and drew parallels between the two women Paul was involved with and his own love relationships while he was living in England. In Paul's Miriam he saw his girlfriend, an Indian nurse named Premi, and in Paul's Clara he saw the older English woman with whom he was, unbeknown to Premi, having an affair. He also identified with Paul's strong ties to his mother. Jaya introduced me to E.M. Forster's *A Passage to India* and explained many things about the Indian way of life. I always spoke English with him and his South African friends, and could thus ensure that my English-speaking persona was intact while keeping in touch with the Swedish part of me through living in a Swedish environment in Lund.

I blissfully enjoyed our relationship, which included dancing on most Saturday nights in the International House common room. Jaya and another Indian South African, Kogs, were on the house entertainment committee and usually chose to play recordings of reggae music, which they had danced to in their hometown, Port Shepstone, on the coast near Durban. Jaya and I would often walk along the beach near Lund, which I believe would have reminded him of his hometown.

All the student rooms at International House included a small bathroom with a toilet, hand basin, and shower. They also contained a tiny cupboard with a hotplate for heating water for coffee or tea. It was expected that the students would go to the ground-floor restaurant for lunch or dinner if they were not having these proper meals somewhere else in the city. The restaurant was named "Finn Inn" after the giant Finn who, according to a Swedish legend, helped construct Lund Cathedral. It offered typical Swedish food such as meatballs and mashed potatoes, at a very reasonable price. Most of the European and American students behaved in the manner expected of them and went to Finn Inn on a regular basis. However, there were many African students living in the house who were not overly fond of the bland Swedish food, and instead wanted to prepare elaborate spicy meals in their rooms. They bought electric rice cookers, an extra hotplate or two, and a small fridge. Cleaning up after a meal was a problem as dishes had to be washed in the tiny bathroom basin and then rinsed under the shower. There were also some plumbing dramas. On one occasion a chicken carcass suddenly appeared in the toilet bowl in my bathroom after someone in a room above me had tried to flush it down the toilet. The entire plumbing system in our wing was blocked and a plumber had to be summoned urgently.

When I first met Jaya, he and his African friends were firmly entrenched in the habit of cooking in their rooms. I often had dinner with them in Jaya's room, where we would sit on cushions on the floor around a low coffee table on which rested plates heaped with saffron rice and various curries. After a month or so, Jaya taught me how to make the curries, and for the first time in my life I was interested in food preparation. Unfortunately, this was also the only time in my life when I felt interested in cooking.

Jaya often told me about his degrading experiences as an Indian growing up in South Africa under the apartheid system. The African National Congress in London had informed him that Sweden was a good place for further study as the student movement in this country was very active and there was a lot of anti-imperialist solidarity with South Africa. Once in Lund, Jaya became an active member of a group of Indian and black South Africans who were working to overthrow apartheid. While we were going out, I didn't realize the extent of his political involvement.

I imagined that Jaya and I would stay together for a long time, perhaps even get married. In fact, we were together less than a year, and I can today pinpoint the beginning of the end. On a typical Saturday night when we were outside International House taking a rest from the strenuous Reggae steps, Jaya turned to me and out of the blue asked: "Would you kiss a white man?"

"Of course," I answered.

"Would you kiss an Indian?"

"You know I would," I said, not knowing where this was going.

"What about a black man, say an African?" he said, testing me.

"No, that might be too different," I replied, without thinking and falling into the trap.

I was a racist but didn't realize this at the time. Jaya would have looked down on me, perhaps even hated me for my answer. He didn't make any comment and I didn't think any more about this episode.

However, soon after this, Jaya started "disappearing" at night. He had given me a key to his room, but he was never there, and his bike was always gone. I remember many nights riding my bike all over Lund looking for his bike parked somewhere. Had he perhaps gone to an all-night political meeting? None of his loyal friends would tell me where he was until one of them finally relented: "He's met an older single mother from Sweden. He prefers her because she has a job and a daughter, and she doesn't focus on him all the time like you do. She is less demanding than you."

I was devastated. I stayed in bed for a week until a friend finally persuaded me to get up.

Looking back, I think the main reason for the breakup was my racist comment, but if I had never made the comment, it wouldn't have made any difference. The relationship would still have ended. It became clear to me that Jaya had only viewed it as one of many "affairs" he had with white women in England and Sweden. It took me a while to realize that he could never truly love a white woman, and sure enough, before long he left the older woman too. Perhaps his series of affairs were a form of unconscious revenge for the way he had been treated in the past under apartheid. It may also be that he was influenced by the fact that his first love, the Indian nurse he had met in London, left him for a white doctor, whom she later married. Predictably, Jaya eventually married an Indian from South Africa. After working in development planning in various African countries, he tragically died after a short illness at the age of only forty-nine.

My relationship with Jaya influenced me both positively and negatively. On the plus side, I became much more politically aware, especially with regard to racism, which led to extensive research into black American literature for my post-graduate studies in English literature. I still have my essay on "The Origin and Use of the Expression Uncle Tom", as well as my assignment on James Baldwin's *Another Country*. On the minus side, after the breakup, for many years I steered away from any serious relationships in order not to get hurt again.

The breakup with Jaya occurred around May 1971. To help me get over him, I moved out of International House into an apartment in a different area of Lund. By September I had finished my undergraduate degree in Russian, English, and political science, and now proceeded with post-graduate studies in English, which I could later count towards the course work component of my Ph.D.

As well as taking on a new apartment, I took on new friends, some of the British and American teachers in the English department at Lund University. At this stage, I also made my first Australian friend, Brian Barnes from Armidale, New South Wales. Brian was a resident in England but traveled to many countries, performing a one-man show, consisting of passages from well-known English literature. Students and teachers in the English department in Lund enjoyed his performances from Dylan Thomas's *Under Milkwood* and *The Diary of Samuel Pepys*. I lost touch with Brian over the years, but recently discovered that in 1962, while still living in Australia, Brian had started the New England Theatre Centre in Armidale as his dream of creating a fully professional country-based touring theater company. I also discovered that he was awarded an MBE (Member of the British Empire) in 2004 for services to English drama.

By October 1971, I still hadn't come to terms with the breakup of my relationship with Jaya. To help me forget, I decided to take a short break from Lund. I found a cheap student flight to New York and asked my father if I could visit him for a couple of weeks. I soon found myself installed in a luxury suite at the Drake Hotel where my father usually stayed on visits to the United Nations when in his role as U.N. mediator in the Middle East. While in New York, I was able to attend "The Family of Man Awards Dinner" on October 26, organized by the Council of Churches of the City of New York. Three bronze medallions for excellence were awarded. My father received an award for his peace efforts in the Middle East. The other two recipients were Joan Cooney for the creation of *Sesame Street* and the Reverend Jesse Jackson for his role in the Civil Rights Movement. The bronze medallion my father received, bearing the ancient Greek inscription, "Pasa Patria," meaning "the whole family," has now found a new home with me in Brisbane. I returned to Lund feeling much better and determined to get on with my life without Jaya.

17. The Career Woman

I never told my parents about Jaya, and they never met him. They didn't visit me while I was a student in Lund, as these years coincided with the busiest years they encountered in their diplomatic life. My father was working in his role as Special Representative of the United Nations Secretary-General to mediate in the Middle East while at the same time continuing as Sweden's Ambassador to the Soviet Union. He had a United Nations jet aircraft assigned to him for his exclusive use, and he practiced one of the early examples of "shuttle diplomacy." He was constantly on the move between the United Nations in New York, his headquarters in Cyprus, and the embassy in Moscow. My mother remained in Moscow, performing her duties as ambassadress, often without the support of my father.

In one of the letters my mother wrote to me from Moscow in 1971, I found the following interesting comment:

> *Ever since I stopped working at the University Library in Lund, I have missed having regular paid work! (...) Although of course in Tehran I also worked at the embassy.*

My mother is referring to my parents' first stay in Iran during World War II.

It's time to look at some more of the letters from Lund. Many of them focus on my mother's career as a librarian. My starting point is Tehran in the early years of the war.

In August 1941 Iran was divided into two zones, one controlled by the Soviet Union and the other by the United Kingdom. Thus, Iran had to break off diplomatic relations with Germany and the Axis Powers. Sweden became a protecting power for Germany and several other foreign states with interests in Iran. In September my father was asked to serve in the Swedish Legation in Tehran since he had a good knowledge of Persian. According to his memoirs, he agreed on the condition that my mother could go with him. *There was no objection to this: she could work in the legation doing clerical work, which was also needed.* They were told that they would be staying for about six months, as by then the war would probably be over. In fact, they ended up staying for four years.

Although my mother had reached a high point in her library career in Lund, she agreed to accompany my father to Tehran, as she was also to be employed in the legation. Moreover, before long she was not just doing the clerical work she had been promised, but more complicated tasks as well. My father only had the help of one attaché who was transferred to Ankara at the end of 1942 without being replaced. As my father wrote in his memoirs, my mother *took part in most of the work, especially with the Bulgarians. She managed this with great elegance with the aid of her good knowledge of Russian.*

In a letter to the Chief Librarian at the University of Lund, my mother commented on the many positive aspects of their life in Tehran:

> *We have an excellent life here, in particular from a financial perspective with free accommodation, car and servants as well as about double the salary compared to at home. If it could continue for a while, Gunnar could pay big instalments on his debts.*
>
> *(…) As far as I am concerned, I am very pleased with my job and my salary. The work is full of variety as I am the only clerk in the B Section here and thus am responsible for*

registration, book-keeping, and passport matters among other things. We are very busy, and both take great pleasure in using our knowledge of Russian as we are visited by about 35 Bulgarians on a daily basis.

Despite the advantages of living in Tehran, my parents were anxious to keep their positions at the Lund University Library. They were granted an extended leave of absence and hoped that their positions would not be negatively affected by their long stay away from Sweden.

I found two later letters from my mother to the Chief Librarian, Lund:

Tehran, 2 October 1942

(…) It was unlucky for me that in March a courier mailbag was lost in Bulgaria. Apparently, it contained (…) a report on the reorganisation of the temporary assistant librarian positions into permanent positions. In her letter, which arrived here in the beginning of September, librarian Signe Carlsson writes that those who held a temporary position on 30 June would automatically become permanent employees. Therefore, I wonder how it is possible that, without informing me who had one of the temporary positions, you could give the position to a less qualified substitute librarian. Minister Pousette has repeatedly written home to the Department of Foreign Affairs explaining that it is essential for me to remain down here at the legation and has especially emphasized that this should not negatively affect my appointment in Sweden. Therefore, I have felt confident that everything had been arranged in the best possible manner. Of course, things down here are excellent in every way (…). However suddenly there might not be any more work due to unforeseen circumstances, and, if

I had known that a permanent position was available, I would have gone home immediately. (…) Gunnar of course still has his research grant (…) but without my income, we cannot exist in Lund.

(…) Our attaché has been transferred to Ankara and Gunnar and I have to handle all the work in the B Section on our own.

Tehran, 5 October 1942

Just now a new letter arrived which completely changed the whole situation. (…) Thank you for your kindness and once again thank you for your kind words which made me very happy.

It seems the situation was rectified, and she would be granted a permanent position on her return to Lund.

On several occasions my mother told me about the missing courier mailbag and how she was worried about her position at the University Library while they were working in Tehran. It's interesting to read about it now in her letters to the Chief Librarian. Although she mentioned the missing mailbag, I had never before understood how much her library work meant to her.

Until I read the letters between my parents, I hadn't realized how much my mother wanted to pursue a career of her own. I had seen her as a diplomatic wife, but never as a working woman. In fact, I felt annoyed that she seemed to have no interest in taking on some paid work after my father retired and they moved to Stockholm. He and I both thought she could have used her excellent Russian knowledge to do some translation work. Now it is clear from the letters that she was very much interested in working at the University

Library in Lund and that she thought it was important for women to work outside the home.

It seems likely that her father influenced her to think in this way. Because his wife, Siri, was unable to look after her children due to her mental illness, Carl Ludvig would have assumed a greater role in their upbringing than was usual for a father during those days. According to his oldest daughter, Essie, he was a devoted father. He played with all five of his daughters and all of them felt loved by him. My mother was perhaps more spoiled than the first four, but this was only natural. As Essie said, *why wouldn't you spoil a girl with curly hair and eyes like stars? In addition, most things came easily to her, and she was almost always kind.* Carl Ludvig also made sure that his girls were intellectually stimulated. They were allowed to read anything on the bookshelves in their home. There is a family joke that when my mother was asked what she was reading at the age of seven, her reply was "Strindberg." Moreover, the daughters were allowed to take part in the discussions when Carl Ludvig invited his students to their home. It was clear that he believed in university education for women. My mother wasn't the only one of his daughters to attend university. Essie studied law and Sonja physiotherapy, although both of them got married before they had a chance to practice their professions. Hella studied pharmacy and pursued this career throughout her life as a single woman.

My mother's excellent linguistic skills were in evidence early on, prompting her father to suggest she translate into Swedish a biography of Isaac Newton written in English by Selig Brodetsky, Professor of Applied Mathematics at Leeds University, which had been published in 1927. The Swedish version was published in Lund in 1928 with a foreword by Carl Ludvig, mentioning the translation by his daughter Agnes Urania. The book is an academic text of 171 pages; my mother was in her late teens when she worked on it and would only have studied English in high school.

While a university student, my mother started working at the same time at the Lund University Library in 1928. According to the library's staff register, she worked there for fourteen years: four of them as casual support and ten as a temporary, then permanent assistant librarian.

My mother's letters demonstrate her serious interest in her work at the University Library and her post-graduate studies. While visiting her sister Essie in August 1931, my mother made the following comment in a letter to my father:

> *Is there no one else but you who misses me at the University Library? (...) It would be wonderful if one in some way was needed upstairs!*

It's evident that she wanted more regular work in the library and hoped to get a temporary rather than mere casual position. This was not only because she found the work interesting, but because she needed the money, as she was unwilling to accept money from my father until they were married, and moreover did not want to accumulate any debts.

My mother's strong belief in the importance of work for women was also evident in a letter to my father, who was doing his military service in Stockholm. One of the female staff in the library had to leave her position even though she had been promised she could stay. This was because one of the male department heads:

> *... went against her with the justification that girls were not suitable for libraries. He conceded that there could be exceptions but that they tended to get married before they had made any valuable contributions. Well, well ...* (May 1932)

In my mother's case, she was allowed to stay on at the library, even after her marriage.

In 1935 the head of the Foreign Department at the Library

seems to have encouraged her to publish a paper on Slavonics. Consequently, she wrote a review of a book in Russian from 1934 about a Soviet polar exploration. In 1936 her four-page article was published in an academic journal in Lund entitled *Geografisk Kronika* (*Geographic Chronicle*).

During most of the four-year period 1936 to 1939, my parents were together in Lund, both working at the University Library and doing research. From time to time my father also went on lecture tours in different parts of Sweden to supplement his income.

Soon after the start of World War II in September 1939, my father was mobilized and ordered to turn up for duty in Ostersund (northern Sweden) by December10. From there he traveled up to the far north of Sweden near the border with Finland where he was assigned as an interpreter of Russian radio transmissions. Then in February 1940 he was transferred to the intelligence service as part of the defense staff in Stockholm.

My mother remained in Lund, continuing to work in the University Library. Once more, her letters to my father demonstrate her serious interest in her career. Commenting on his work in northern Sweden, she wrote:

> *Your time is not wasted and perhaps you will get a better job after this. As long as it's not too far away from the University Library I will be pleased.*

Her feelings of being unfairly treated as a woman also come to the surface when she said:

> *It's unfair that lazy people get promoted while hard-working capable people have to stay where they are out of pity. At the University Library I have definitely done 10 times as much during these 12 years as the mentioned gentlemen.* (February 2, 1940)

In October 1940 my father was still mobilized in Stockholm, but he was soon appointed to the Swedish Legation in Ankara, where the National Defense paid half his salary for his services as military attaché, and the Department of Foreign Affairs the other half for his services as a diplomatic attaché. He left Lund for Turkey on November 3, 1940, together with my mother. They kept their apartment and housekeeper in Lund and my mother was granted a leave of absence from the library. Sometime earlier she had embarked on a Ph.D. in Russian and planned to work on her thesis in Turkey. (This Ph.D. was never completed.)

My mother did not stay long in Ankara. By the end of January 1941, she left in order to return to her University Library position. My father remained in Ankara for another three months. Once back in Lund, my mother's letters to him reflected an even stronger commitment to her library work, or some other kind of work. She expressed a wish to work in the Swedish Legation in Ankara if my father didn't return soon. Her increasing independence and self-confidence were both evident. Thus, on February 7, 1941 she wrote:

> *Actually, I am very happy to be home. Of course, in many ways it was charming in Turkey and I very much miss Ankara "by night". However, you see there were drawbacks for me in not having a job and kind of being on the outside of everything. If I am going to travel out again, it will have to be on the condition that I am allowed to help … When I am on my own, I manage very well such as now on the journey home. But when I'm with you, I become some kind of second-rate figure who lives under your shadow. This sounds unkind but is unfortunately true.*

A letter from a few days later, February 19, 1941, reinforces the points she made above:

> *(…) I have been given a very fine task at the library, namely, to make a "catalogue of slogans." To begin with I will be*

working on it for 6 months and then we will see. (…) This is apparently the end of my free life with no hope of getting a leave of absence from time to time and traveling to you to be a wife living in luxury. But you will come home to me instead, won't you?

I am happy to have my work and to feel that I am doing something useful. In Turkey I always felt that I was in the way and good for nothing. Except to drink and dance …

And a few days later on February 23, 1941 she wrote:

At the moment I feel pretty indispensable in the University Library on account of the slogan catalogue. The work is considered a very good qualification and it is work that will be relevant over time. And I am really interested in it and feel like a human being rather than like the inferior creature I most often (forgive me!) felt like in Ankara. I hate feeling so superfluous and "in the way" as I did there!

The excerpts from these three letters all show the strength of my mother's feelings. There is no doubt that she firmly believed in the importance of working and being independent.

My father returned from Ankara to Lund in April as planned. In his memoirs, he mentions that he *didn't have the slightest thought of definitely giving up* (his university position). In a letter from the end of March 1941, my mother mentioned that they would perhaps now be living in Lund for the remainder of their lives. However, fate had something else in store when they were asked to serve in the Swedish Legation in Tehran during World War II.

I feel proud of my mother after reading the many letters which reflect her strong views on the importance for women to have a career or at least some kind of work outside the home. I admire her for working at the University Library, even returning from Ankara by herself in order to continue her career, and later for working in the Swedish Legation in Tehran during World War II. It's amazing to think of my parents working side by side there during those four years with little help. According to my father's memoirs, they resided on their own in the abandoned German Embassy. He also described how they had to deal with all the belongings left behind when the Germans had to leave the city. All of the work my mother did over many years took place at a time when most married women would have been content in their role as housewives.

In retrospect, I now remember how, when I was a child, my mother tried to instil in me an interest in a professional career. One of my earliest memories from Stockholm which has come to the surface is my mother handing me a medical encyclopedia and telling me to look at the sometimes-confronting photos of various diseases and medical conditions. I would have been about four and not yet able to read. I think she secretly hoped that this would stimulate my interest and that I would become a (medical) doctor. For my tenth birthday in Washington, she gave me an "invisible man," which was a kind of human model made of transparent plastic and accompanied with all his vital organs in separate bags. These had to be assembled and glued in the correct place inside him. In other words, it was a lesson in anatomy disguised as a toy. It may also be that she wanted to encourage me to become a veterinarian because when I was a child, she always gave me stuffed animals rather than dolls. This could have been one of her own aspirations, hinted at in a letter to my father in India just before my birth in Sweden:

If I were to embark on a new career, I would have a large kennel with different animals ... or else I would become a veterinarian. It is also worthwhile. (March 1, 1949)

After reading my mother's letters, I have got to know my mother as a career woman and have become fully aware of how much a career and meaningful work meant to her. I now feel that my mother's influence on me in this regard was much stronger than I had previously believed. Why did I choose to focus on the portrayal of strong female characters in the fiction of the female writer Henry Handel Richardson (pseudonym for Ethel Florence Lindsay Richardson) for my Ph.D. thesis? Why had I always believed it was important for women to be highly educated and engaged in interesting work? This could be the influence of the excellent female teachers at National Cathedral School, whom I regarded as role models, or the influence of living in Sweden, where it is important that women work to fulfil their social responsibility. However, it also seems likely that my mother influenced me to seriously consider the position of women in society, even though she hadn't been able to provide me with a model of herself as a career woman after I was born.

18. A Major Turning Point: Townsville

By May 1973, I had spent more than four years in Lund and my parents became worried that I seemed to be just marking time there. I had finished my undergraduate degree as well as a year of course work in English at post-graduate level. Unsure how to proceed, I had then enrolled in economic history and an introductory course in law. (At this time there were no fees for university study in Sweden.) My father now intervened, and through his contacts got me a position in Handelsbanken, one of the major commercial banks in Stockholm. There I was to learn some basic banking skills before using my knowledge of Russian to help set up a branch office for the bank in Moscow. Once settled in Stockholm, I was again unhappy; I now realize that this was mainly because I had yet again lost part of my identity, namely my English-speaking self.

I persevered in my banking role for just under a year, but I had no aptitude for figures and no real interest in financial matters. Thus, when the opening of the Moscow office was delayed, I asked to change to part-time, less qualified work so that I could pursue Ph.D. studies in English at Stockholm University. Some of my colleagues in the bank were horrified that I preferred a future as an academic, and tried to persuade me to stay. But my mind was made up.

Again, my life was back in balance. I did mundane banking tasks using Swedish with my colleagues from 9 a.m. to 1 p.m., and then took the underground out to the university to attend lectures and tutorials held in English in the afternoon. In those days, the Ph.D. in Sweden was comprised of 50 percent course work (covering vast areas of British and American literature) and of 50 percent work on researching and writing a thesis. I had, in fact, started on the course work in Lund and now continued on from there.

Although I was quite happy with this solution to my identity problem, my "American" English-speaking self was again getting stronger than my Swedish self, even though I was living in a Swedish environment, and I was actively looking for more ways to get in touch with this stronger self. There was, for example, an English pub near where I lived, which I frequently visited. I also took several boat trips to England in order to buy books needed for my Ph.D. I could buy these much more cheaply there than in Sweden and thus actually ended up saving money in this way.

I had started looking into training as a radio operator on a ship that would take me away from Sweden and hopefully into an English-speaking environment, when a golden opportunity presented itself at the end of 1975. Professor Colin Roderick from James Cook University, Townsville, Australia, visited the English Department at Stockholm University. He told us about the Australian European Awards Program through which a small number of students from various European countries would receive a full scholarship for a year in order to complete a master's degree in Australia. This was an initiative of the then Prime Minister, Gough Whitlam. The aim of the program was for the students to return to their own countries when the year was up and spread Australian culture in Europe. However, this backfired more than once, as students tended to marry Australians and stay on in Australia. I applied and in February 1976 was finally informed that I had received one of the awards and had a place at James Cook University to study Australian literature.

I think deep down I had always had a longing to visit Australia. On one of my annual summer holiday boat trips from the U.S.A.

to Sweden with my mother, two fellow passengers seated at the captain's table with us were a Mr. Dinsmore and his wife. He was a retired American film maker who was now making his way around the world by ship, filming all the stopovers on the way. Mr. Dinsmore let me look at the extensive footage he had taken so far, which covered places in South America, Africa, and Asia. I don't remember any of what I saw regarding these. However, he also had some film from Australia, and there was a short footage of his wife in Sydney holding a koala, which is etched in my memory. Was this just because the koala was exotic for me, or was it a sign that I had a secret longing to visit Australia one day in the future?

Studying in Townsville from March to November in 1976 was one of the best times of my life. Keeping the Swedish part of me intact was no problem because I had a part-time job teaching Swedish to a small group of adults at James Cook. In this way, I also discovered my love of teaching, which eventually led to a career in teaching English as a foreign language to adults. My very generous scholarship included funds for travel within Australia, so I was thus able to visit Swedish friends at the Embassy in Canberra and also the Swedish department at Melbourne University. On a visit to Sydney, I admired the beautiful Opera House, designed by the Danish architect Jørn Utzon. I was amazed to discover that its curved shell-shaped roof was covered by ceramic tiles from Hoganas, a small town six kilometers north of Viken, where I had spent most of my summers. Of course, I also wrote weekly letters in Swedish to my parents. In addition, the year 1976 saw the Swedish pop group ABBA at the height of their popularity in Australia, so frequently hearing "Fernando" and other ABBA tunes while being immersed in an English-speaking country made me feel that my two personae had truly merged.

The year in Townsville was a major turning point in my life. A friend of mine once commented on how happy I sounded in my letters from Townsville. She was right about how I felt and there were several reasons for this. First, getting the scholarship was something I had achieved on my own merits and not because I was the daughter of Gunnar Jarring, as had been the case with the bank position.

Moreover, I loved the warm climate in Townsville and its tropical scenery. The city is situated on the east coast, north of the Tropic of Capricorn. I found it beautiful and exotic and a very welcome change from the cold wintry Sweden I had left behind. I loved looking at the palm trees along the Strand and on visits to nearby Magnetic Island, a short ferry ride from Townsville. Every morning I would stand on the balcony of my room at University Hall, the residential college where I was staying, and look out at Castle Hill, a small rocky outcrop in the distance. Every day I would wake up to a blue sky and perfect temperature hovering around 30ºC. At night I would often go for walks around the campus and look up at constellations and stars that were different from those in the northern hemisphere. I felt like I had landed in the middle of a scene from one of my favorite musicals, *South Pacific*. I don't recall needing a sweater or catching a cold even once during my whole time in Townsville. In Sweden, on the other hand, I had always suffered from the freezing weather and tended to have a cold or sore throat for six months of the year.

The next reason why I felt happy relates to overcoming my fears. I had always tended to feel anxious and scared when encountering situations that could prove to be dangerous, even if only slightly so. This was probably due to my mother being overly protective towards me and passing some of her own fears onto me while I was growing up. Before my departure for Australia, I visited the Australian Embassy in Stockholm and was bombarded with warnings about the venomous snakes and spiders as well as sharks, which were part of Australian life, especially in a remote place like Townsville. At this point I nearly changed my mind about accepting the scholarship.

For a year or two I also suffered from an extreme fear of flying, caused by a trip to Moscow to visit my parents traveling on the Russian airline Aeroflot. I can still remember the flight in detail. We were taxiing along the runway at Arlanda Airport, Stockholm, and had almost reached the point from which we would begin our take-off. Suddenly we were making our way back to the terminal and were told to disembark. An anonymous person had phoned in to say that there was a bomb on board our plane. In those days, the early 1970s, security was not very sophisticated, and baggage was not put through x-ray machines. Instead, all our bags were lined up on the tarmac and we had to point out which ones were ours. Once claimed, the bags were loaded back onto the plane. After an hour or so, there were no unclaimed bags left on the tarmac and the airport authorities were satisfied that it had all been a hoax. I got back into my seat near the front of the plane, and we were once again ready to take off. We were in the air and the seat belt signs had just been switched off, when there was a loud bang. Believing it to be caused by the bomb which had failed to be discovered, the overweight female flight attendants threw themselves down in the aisle screaming. The cockpit door opened, the captain rushed out and seemed to be checking that the wing on the left-hand side of the plane was intact. He then silently retreated to the cockpit. For the next two hours until we reached Moscow, we were given no information about what had just occurred.

Once we landed, we found out it was a lightning strike that had caused an electrical fault. The plane was unable to continue on its route to Singapore. I was extremely happy to be on the ground and refused to fly again for years. During this period when I visited my parents in Moscow, I would travel by train via Poland.

Thus, to take up my studies in Townsville, I had to overcome my exaggerated fear of flying. I took a boat from Sweden to London and then prepared for the 24-hour flight to Brisbane on Qantas. I remember how nervous I felt about flying as well as setting off into the unknown by myself. It turned out to be a smooth, pleasant flight with a couple of short stop-offs to refuel. By the time I arrived in Brisbane my fears had disappeared. I was cured and went on to happily take other flights within Australia during my scholarship year. In fact, it would be true to say that during that year, I lived without anxiety or fear for the first time that I could remember. I traveled over 1000 kilometers by car from Townsville to Brisbane, albeit as a passenger, as I didn't have a driver's license yet. I struggled on and off a ski lift outside Canberra and swam in water that I knew to be inhabited by sharks. It was all very liberating and made me feel happy.

The year in Townsville was also an important milestone on my way to becoming independent of my parents. I had left Lund for my banking job in 1973. Soon after this, my parents retired from the diplomatic service and returned to Stockholm, where my father had been offered a position as consultant to the Johnson Group of Companies. Thus, for the first time since the age of fourteen, I was living in the same city as my parents, although not with them but in my own flat, which was near them. Suddenly I found myself having dinner at their apartment on many nights, as I found it difficult to refuse my mother's invitations to stop by. More and more I was losing the independence I had built up for over ten years. I knew I had to escape in order to grow up and become my own person, so I took this step by spending the academic year 1976 in Australia. If I hadn't left for Townsville, I would have risked being pulled back into the life I led when I was fourteen, remaining a child rather than becoming an independent adult. I sometimes think I would never have married and would instead have ended up living next door to my parents and looking after them in their old age as their ever-dutiful but not very happy daughter.

19. The Wedding

During the year in Townsville, I met the man who was to become my husband. Two years younger than me, Steve was already a lecturer in law at James Cook University at the age of twenty-five. I had absolutely no expectation that I would meet a suitable single man in Townsville, and I think that's often the time when something like that suddenly happens. Without being fully aware of it, I was finally ready for a real relationship again after Jaya. There was an immediate physical as well as intellectual connection between Steve and me. I walked into his study at University Hall, where we were both living, and saw many of the same works of English literature that I had on my shelves at home in Sweden. From my observations of people around me, when you meet the right person, things usually move along quickly. When my scholarship year was up, I returned to Stockholm and resumed my part-time bank job and Ph.D. studies, but after about six months Steve followed. We got married in Viken's church in August 1977.

My parents met Steve only a few days before the wedding, and I could tell that they liked him very much from the start. My mother quickly told me that he seemed to be someone you could depend on through thick and thin, and she was right about that. I think Steve immediately appreciated my mother's ironic sense of humor and didn't take offence at her comment about the watch he had bought for me as an engagement present. He had spent a lot of time and money choosing a gold Omega watch with a rectangular face and Roman numerals with a black crocodile leather band. "Oh, is it real gold?" my mother asked while scrutinizing the watch with her myopic gaze. For his part, my father apologized to Steve for the fact that we were only having frozen shrimps and ready-made meatballs for our first dinner together, which was all my mother could prepare without domestic help.

Steve's parents and his best friend, Robert, flew over from Brisbane for the wedding. Because there were so few guests from Steve's side, we decided to make the church ceremony very small with just my parents, my friend Asa, and a handful of relatives attending from my side. We also decided that Steve and I would walk down the aisle together rather than my father giving me away. The priest was my confirmation priest, Lars Vogelius, who performed the ceremony in English. The sun was shining and the church looked beautiful with its plain white walls, pale blue, barrel-vaulted ceiling, and the model sailing ships hanging down on either side of the nave. The ships were relics from the past when Viken had been a thriving fishing village and later an important boat building center.

After the ceremony, there was a small reception at my parents' house where we drank Veuve Cliquot champagne, before we set off in a taxi with our parents and two best friends for the ferry in Helsingborg, which would take us across to Denmark for a sumptuous wedding dinner. I'll never forget how people on the ferry pointed at me in my simple wedding dress, still carrying my bouquet of small red roses and white carnations. They cried: "Look, a bride, a bride!" Because Viken's Hotel had closed down, the venue chosen for the dinner was Hotel Marienlyst, a short stroll from Hamlet's castle in Helsingør, where we had disembarked from the ferry. It was considered the best hotel in Denmark, and in the 1890s had been awarded the title "Royal", due to its popularity with the royal family. During World War II it had been the local headquarters for the Nazis during their occupation of Denmark.

The wedding took place on a Saturday and on the following day there was a larger reception in my parents' garden in Viken with many friends and relatives. One of the guests was a classmate from Sigtuna, who happened to look a lot like the English actor Michael York. I still remember how my mother-in-law took me aside and whispered, "How could you choose to marry my son when you could have chosen that handsome man?" I assured her that I much preferred Steve's brown eyes and dark hair, finding him much more handsome than any blond, blue-eyed Swede.

During the days after we were married, I couldn't stop looking at my hand with its gold band and feeling how strange and wonderful it was to be married. We had exchanged rings in the church after they were blessed by the priest. In Sweden it is customary for both husbands and wives to wear a wedding ring throughout their married life. After just a few days, Steve managed to lose his ring in the washing machine at my parents' apartment in Stockholm. I managed to retrieve it, but soon noticed that his hand was again bare. It took a while before he explained that many men in Australia don't wear a wedding ring, so his ring has stayed in a box from that time. This was an early difference that I noted between Sweden and Australia.

A few days after the wedding, we found ourselves on our honeymoon exploring Finland, yet another Scandinavian country. Together with Asa and Robert, we took the ferry from Stockholm to Helsinki, where we stayed in a central hotel for two nights before the return crossing to Sweden. This trip was unfortunately marred by my handbag being stolen in a bar on the return ferry. Being young and foolish, I had left it on the floor next to our table when I got up to dance and it was quickly snapped up by a thief looking for just such opportunities. This person would have taken out the cash and then thrown the bag overboard, as witnessed by Robert and

Asa who were out on the deck. Unfortunately, my bag contained not just the keys to my flat in Stockholm, but also Steve's passport! Thus, when we got back to Stockholm, we had to spend many hours visiting the Australian Embassy getting a new passport, as well as visa and work permit for Steve before we were due to leave for London at the beginning of September.

20. Transition Years in London

We spent six years in London, where Steve first studied for his master's degree in law at University College London (UCL) and then worked as a lawyer for Slaughter and May, a large commercial law firm in the City. I did research in the vast, domed reading room of the British Library (then part of the British Museum) for my Ph.D. on the Australian writer Henry Handel Richardson, who had lived in England for most of her adult life.

On the political front, those years we lived in London (1977–83) were filled with drama. Britain was in deep recession and in the grip of an economic and social crisis. Unemployment was about to reach three million people. During the 1970s there were frequent blackouts when the government decided to cut power in order to conserve coal after the miners had gone on strike. Many older London residents were reminded of the Blitz during World War II and complained bitterly. There were many IRA bombings, some close to where we lived in Bloomsbury. In December 1978 three bombs went off near the British Museum and in 1981 there were bombs in Oxford Street. Whenever we entered a cinema or department store, we had to present our bags to be security checked. April to June 1982 saw the dispute between the UK and Argentina over the Falklands. Margaret Thatcher was prime minister from 1979 to 1990 and thus during most of our London years. In July 1981, I vividly remember standing outside St. Paul's Cathedral, listening to the wedding of Charles and Diana which was being broadcast over loudspeakers.

In London I again found the perfect balance between my two personae. I was living in an English-speaking environment and spent my days reading and writing in English for my Ph.D. thesis. At the same time, I was enrolled for my doctorate at Stockholm University and later Lund University, and had to visit my current supervisor in Sweden at certain times during the year. I would usually combine these visits with seeing my parents in Stockholm or Viken and they would also visit us in London from time to time.

My Swedish persona was further developed through teaching Swedish at the Polytechnic of Central London in the evening, as well as giving private lessons. Not being a trained language teacher at this stage, I tended to teach the way I myself had been taught foreign languages, French and German, at boarding school in Sweden, which meant using the grammar/translation method. This involved using English to explain very detailed grammar rules to my students, giving them lots of Swedish words with their meanings in English, and then getting them to translate increasingly complicated passages of text from Swedish into English. In this manner my students acquired a good understanding of Swedish, but they were given little opportunity to speak or listen to it. Although my students may have missed out on being taught according to the most current teaching methods, they seemed to enjoy my teaching. For my part, I enjoyed watching their progress and for me it was also a wonderful way to expand my knowledge of my first language.

A few years later when I undertook my diploma in education and my master's degree in TESOL (Teaching English to Speakers of Other Languages), I learned other more communicative and effective ways to teach a language, for example, teaching according to social functions such as asking questions or expressing disagreement. There was also the well-known PPP approach, where a grammatical structure or vocabulary item is <u>presented</u>, the students <u>practice</u> it by repeating after the teacher, and finally the students <u>produce</u> their own versions of the target language. The approaches to language teaching I learned later on have the advantage that students gain a much more active knowledge of the language: they can speak and write it, not just understand it when reading or listening.

Apart from my students, we didn't get to know many English people while we were living in London. This was probably because many of them seemed to be reserved and difficult to approach. But it is also likely to be because most of the people we came across were not British. During the first couple of years, we stayed in William Goodenough House, now Goodenough College, in Mecklenburgh Square. This was a place that provided accommodation for postgraduate students and their families from Commonwealth countries, the United States, and the European Union. Many of Steve's fellow students in the UCL master's program were also from the Commonwealth. I was not attending any seminars for my Ph.D. in London as I was enrolled for my doctorate in Sweden. Instead, I was isolated, pursuing my research in the British Library and later typing up chapters at home on a portable typewriter. Although we did later become acquainted with some young English lawyers when Steve was working for the law firm, most of the people we met in England were Australian or Swedish contacts of mine, some of which I made through part-time work as an administrative assistant at the Swedish Embassy from March to May in 1980.

Interestingly, two English people I did meet were both famous British novelists. When I studied English at Lund University, one of my favorite authors was Margaret Drabble, who even visited the English Department in Lund to talk about her books. She wore a wide-brimmed hat and had all the male lecturers competing to show her around. Someone told me that Drabble taught English literature somewhere in London so I attended a short course on love and marriage in some selected novels taught by her. A few years later I took part in a Russian class to brush up my language skills from the Lund and Moscow days. It was held at the Polytechnic of Central London where I taught Swedish, and I was surprised to find myself sitting next to Doris Lessing, who was attending the class with her son. Both Margaret Drabble and Doris Lessing turned out to be quiet and unassuming. I suspect that they needed a break from their hours of isolated work as writers and had chosen to spend some time teaching or learning as a way of socializing and relaxing, or perhaps even to get ideas for their next novels.

For me, the London years were a time of transition before moving from my life in Europe to my new life in Australia. I got to know many Australians who were studying in London, and we also had many visits from Steve's family and friends from Brisbane. On a regular basis we visited Australia House to see Australian films, which served as a further introduction to Australian society and values. Many excellent movies were produced at this time; I particularly remember *The Getting of Wisdom,* based on the novel by Henry Handel Richardson, *My Brilliant Career*, and *Gallipoli*. I found it interesting to note the essential difference between Australia with its egalitarianism and mateship, and England with its class distinctions and hierarchies. However, it was difficult to reconcile this with the fact that Queen Elizabeth II was Head of State for both Great Britain and Australia. How could the egalitarian Australians share the same Head of State with the class-conscious British?

In March 1980 we were given the opportunity to see Her Majesty the Queen in person when she visited the Commonwealth and other overseas students in Mecklenburgh Square. She was visiting in her dual capacity as Head of the Commonwealth and Head of State for the United Kingdom. She was dressed in a dark blue woolen suit with a large blue sapphire and diamond brooch on her left shoulder. I was surprised by how small she was compared to how I had imagined her from the images in the media. We were divided into nationality groups consisting of students from different countries, the Africans in brightly colored national dress, and were told to form a large circle along the walls of the dining hall. The Queen moved slowly from group to group, asking questions and making small talk: "Where are you from?" "What are you studying?" "Are you happy here?" In total she spent about an hour with the groups before she was ushered away. Even though the conversations were only superficial, the fact that she had spoken to us left a lasting impression, and for a long time afterwards I had recurring dreams in which the Queen made an appearance. Many years later when I attended the ceremony to become an Australian citizen in Brisbane, my eyes were drawn to the portrait of Queen Elizabeth in the City Hall, and I was reminded of her visit to us in London.

The London years were not only a time of transition into the future, but also a time to reconnect with the past. Two examples of this were to be found among my Swedish students. One of them was Countess Jill Bernadotte, an English woman, who in 1981 had married the Swedish Count Bertil Bernadotte, and for this reason wanted to learn some Swedish. Bertil Bernadotte is a cousin of the Swedish King and the son of Count Folke Bernadotte, who like my father had been appointed United Nations mediator in the Middle East. He was assassinated in 1948 by the militant Zionist group, Lehi.

Another of my students was Jaya's young Indian wife, Premi. She didn't attend very many lessons, but when I ran into her and Jaya on a London street, I realized who she was. They invited Steve and me for dinner, but I politely refused their invitation, not wishing to be reminded of a part of the past which I had unequivocally left behind. I assumed Premi wanted to learn Swedish because they were moving back to Sweden after a time in London.

Other connections with the past were related to the diplomatic service. During my year in Australia in 1976, I met Per Lind, who was Sweden's Ambassador in Canberra. His daughter, Birgitta, had been my classmate at boarding school in Sigtuna and had settled outside Wellington after marrying a New Zealander. Per Lind had now been appointed Ambassador to the United Kingdom and I met him again when he gave a party for Birgitta, who was visiting from New Zealand. The party was held at the Ambassador's residence in Portland Place with its magnificent eighteenth-century interiors by Robert Adam.

On one of my parents' visits to London, we caught up with the Jacobsen family. Frithjof Jacobsen had been Norway's Ambassador to the Soviet Union at the same time as my father and was now Ambassador to the United Kingdom. I knew his two daughters well from Moscow and enjoyed meeting them again. Ambassador Jacobsen invited us for lunch at the Trafalgar Tavern situated on the bank of the Thames at Greenwich. The tavern opened in 1837 and had been frequented by Charles Dickens, who set the wedding breakfast in *Our Mutual Friend* there. We ate whitebait in a light, crispy batter for which the tavern was famous. After lunch we drove back to the Ambassador's residence in Kensington Palace Gardens for afternoon tea, during which my parents reminisced with the Jacobsens about their Moscow days.

My parents were staying at Claridge's in Brook Street, Mayfair and we had lunch with them in the dining room, which at that time was painted in a palette of muted creams, pinks, and greys. We were served English roast beef that was carved at the table from a gleaming silver trolley. After lunch we stopped at an antique shop in Brook Street and my mother purchased a matching pair of China Pekingese dogs seated on pale blue and white striped cushions with gilt tassels. The golden-brown Pekes with bulging eyes are now staring up at me from my desk in Brisbane and are a memento of that happy London visit by my parents.

My mother's love for dogs had moved on to smaller breeds that were more suitable, given her age and the fact that they were living in an apartment in central Stockholm most of the year. She had settled on the Pekingese, a breed that to me seemed more like a cat than a dog. Mingka, and later Ming, became the object of her affection in her later life and accompanied her everywhere.

21. Anger

Our first five years in London were filled with sight-seeing and theater and restaurant visits. We were also busy settling into our own small one-bedroom apartment at Trinity Court in Gray's Inn Road, around the corner from Mecklenburgh Square where we had previously lived. It had a nice view overlooking St. Andrew's Gardens but was quite cold in winter, as it had no effective heating and no double-glazed windows. Parking was impossible, but we were happy to save money by not having a car. For the same reason, we didn't have a washing machine, or a telephone. Instead, we relied on public transport and taxis, which were inexpensive and readily available, laundromats, and public telephones. Mobile phones were still unheard of.

My early married life in England was a time when I should have been ecstatically happy, but I also found myself at times confronted by strong feelings of anger I didn't know I possessed. I remember one evening when my husband, who was then working as a lawyer in the City, came home late. We were living in our small flat in Gray's Inn Road. He had been held up by a meeting at the office and hadn't been able to contact me to say he would be late.

Usually, we had dinner at 8. It was now after 9. I had covered our steaks in the frying pan and had put the salad back in the fridge. I had also done all the ironing. As I now waited, I felt as though a big black hole was opening up inside me. I felt abandoned and became increasingly angry. When Steve finally walked in, I had already decided that he didn't love me anymore.

"I've been waiting and waiting. Why didn't you tell me you would be late? You obviously don't care about me," I said in an accusing tone of voice.

"The meeting was called at the last minute, and I couldn't get out of it. I couldn't call you."

"No, you lied to me. You said you would be here on time, and you weren't. You don't love me."

When I got no response from Steve, I had by now worked myself up into such a state that I threw one of our best wedding presents, a beautiful multi-colored crystal bowl, at him. In tears I watched it crash into pieces at his feet.

Lying awake well into the night, I thought about how our marriage, like the bowl, had been smashed before being given a chance. However, my husband is a kind, forgiving man and when the sun shone onto our breakfast table the next morning, and the little flat was bright and cheery after the cold, dark night, he forgave me, and our life continued as before.

However, over the coming years many more bouts of anger occurred, usually triggered by trivial things. I was unable to understand or stop my feelings of anger, just like a depressed person is unable to stop himself from suddenly bursting into tears. My husband never knew when to expect an outburst from me. It would be a few years before I realized why I was so angry and could put a stop to my destructive behavior.

There was an explanation for this anger which gradually came to light. Clearly, I was strongly tied to my mother and would have been upset when she left me behind at boarding school in Washington when she departed for Moscow. I seemed to have accepted that my father had to follow his career and move when he was told to by the Department of Foreign Affairs. However, at the time I didn't understand why my mother had to go with him and without me. I now realize that she had no choice. As a diplomat's wife, she had to follow her husband in accordance with his current posting, but then I must have wondered why she couldn't stay with me in Washington, at least until the end of the school year in June. At the stage when I was left alone in the States, I was still overly tied to my mother and hadn't yet started to break free from her. I felt that she had abandoned me and didn't love me. What I didn't realize until much later was that I had felt very angry with my mother for leaving me behind and had repressed these feelings. They later came back and made problems for me when I found myself inexplicably angry with my husband during the early years of our marriage.

After many hours of therapy in both London and later in Brisbane, I finally came to terms with my feelings of anger towards my mother. Perhaps I felt that as a teenage daughter, I should have been the one initiating the break and not the other way around. (No doubt, I had also been angry with her when I was a young child and felt she was neglecting me and not appreciating all my efforts to please her.)

I must have initially shown my anger, because years later when my friend Anna and I were reminiscing about our years in Washington, she told me I had been very angry when I had been left at the boarding school. I found it hard to believe her because I had not only bottled up my feelings since that time, but had totally pushed them out of my conscious mind to the extent that I had no memory of how I had felt. I can remember my mother leaving home in our car with the dog and later Pertti, the chauffeur, driving me to the boarding school, but I can't remember feeling angry, or feeling anything at all for that matter.

I lived through those boarding school months in Washington and another four years at the Swedish boarding school, going through all the motions of living: getting good report cards, making friends, growing up, but not feeling very deeply. I felt sad for a few hours on the day my mother left me at my Swedish boarding school, but my capacity to experience strong emotions of any kind seemed to have been suppressed from the time my mother left me at the school in Washington. I must have decided that if I didn't allow myself to feel too deeply, I wouldn't be hurt again.

Admittedly, I had been in love with Jaya, but when this led to being rejected once again, I was devastated and only allowed myself to have relationships which didn't pose any threat to me in terms of my becoming involved and having strong feelings. I couldn't stop myself from falling in love with Jaya, but after our breakup, I seemed once more to be able to control my feelings in the same way I coped after what I perceived as my mother's abandonment of me all those years ago in Washington. It was easy to remain independent and "unfeeling" when living alone in Lund and later Stockholm.

During the years after Washington, I would describe my relationship with my mother as friendly but not very warm. During my many visits to Moscow, we played bridge together or went to the Bolshoi Theatre to see a popular ballet, sitting in the front row seats reserved for members of the diplomatic corps, but I don't remember confiding in her or asking her for advice. I believed I had separated from her and had escaped from her influence over me.

But marriage made all the difference to my suppressed emotions. I had loved my mother and now I allowed myself to love again. But when I felt rejected by my husband (for example when he came home late), this reminded me of my mother's "abandonment" of me. My feelings of anger towards her had finally surfaced after many years and were now projected onto him.

Understanding that I was angry because of my mother's "abandonment" of me was not difficult, especially for someone like me who tends to analyse and intellectualize my feelings, but it was not enough to make me stop feeling angry. I also had to get rid of my anger by reliving it in therapy, and this was much harder. My first psychotherapist was a West Indian man who lived in an outer suburb of London. He saw his clients in his bedroom, or perhaps it was a spare room, in a tiny flat near the railway station. He told me to sit on the floor and punch some large cushions as hard as I could while repeating, "He [my husband] is not my mother." This did not seem to have much effect on me. I didn't fare much better later in Brisbane. My first therapist here tried to make me relive my anger by telling me things like "Your mother always wanted a son not a daughter." Even before I read my mother's letters, I intuitively knew that this wasn't true. I never managed to feel angry during any of our sessions. My last therapist spent a lot of time, paid for by me, telling me about the problems she was having coming to terms with growing old! Despite my not very successful attempts to use therapy to relive my feelings, after some time I had apparently worked through them enough to be able to stop feeling angry with my mother and could stop my inappropriate behavior towards my husband.

22. Moving Downunder

We were on the whole living happily in our small flat in the center of London when our first daughter, Celia, arrived in November 1982.

We stayed on in London for another year so that I could finish my thesis. I was lucky that Celia was a very good baby, allowing me long stretches of time to work on my Ph.D. while she slept, and even giving me time to give some private Swedish lessons in the flat to earn some extra money. However, it was hard at times living in such cramped, often chilly, quarters with a baby, no car, and doing the washing at a launderette.

We moved to Brisbane at the end of 1983 after I had defended my doctorate at Lund University in September. Steve had a position waiting for him as a lecturer in Law at Queensland Institute of Technology (later Queensland University of Technology). He decided to pursue an academic career and practice law part-time.

Life with a baby was certainly much simpler in Brisbane. After a few weeks of living with Steve's parents, we moved into our first house in Antill Street, Wilston, on the north side of the river. It was a typical Queensland timber house perched on timber stumps, with three bedrooms. We could appreciate the size of the house and the large garden surrounding it after our small, but cozy London flat. In 1985 our second daughter, Claire, was born.

Many things about Brisbane appealed to me from the start: living in a house rather than an apartment, being able to easily admire the moon and stars from our backyard and see the horizon from one of the many hills in our neighborhood, the warm tropical climate, and the unusual exotic animals such as possums and lizards. To me it was amazing to live in a relatively large city with all its benefits, while at the same time feeling so close to nature. Above all, I was impressed by the friendliness of the Australian people and their tolerant treatment of foreigners. It was very easy to feel at home here. Living in Brisbane has turned out to be the longest I have ever lived in one city and one country.

People have often asked me how I could enjoy life in Brisbane after so many years of privileged diplomatic life and our years in cosmopolitan London. It's true that when we first moved to Brisbane, it was a provincial town, and this only started to change after the World Exposition was held here in 1988. It was the naturalness and simplicity compared to the artificiality and sophistication of diplomatic life that appealed to me. Where I was used to luxurious bathrooms and kitchens, I was fascinated by our first Brisbane house which was from the 1920's and had only been partially renovated when we bought it. The cast-iron bathtub was still in its original position, and there was a hard ceramic kitchen sink, in which I inevitably managed to break countless glasses while doing the washing up. I found it quaint that my mother-in-law, a doctor's wife, still wore a hat and gloves to visit the city center, just as my mother had done in the 1950s. It was like going back in time, and I found it interesting.

When I first arrived in Brisbane, I thought I would have little difficulty securing a position as a university tutor or lecturer with my Ph.D. in Australian literature. However, already by this time, the mid 1980s, the study of literature was beginning to be phased out and gradually replaced by communication and to some extent linguistics. Like many others, I was unable to find a suitable job where

I could use my Ph.D. Instead, I enrolled in a Diploma of Education at the University of Queensland with a view to becoming a high school teacher. My two curriculum subjects were English and ESL (English as a Second Language). Lacking the essential skills to discipline students for misbehavior, I don't think I would have been a very good high school teacher.

Soon after finishing my diploma, I secured a casual job teaching English to overseas students at what was to become the Institute of Continuing and TESOL Education (ICTE) at the University of Queensland. At my job interview the director, Christine Bundesen, and I discovered that we were the same age and had lived in Washington D.C. at the same time, although we had attended different private schools. Her father was stationed there during his military career. During the interview, Christine and I shared memories of having been invited to the White House. She remembered attending the traditional Easter Egg Roll on the lawn, to which the children and grandchildren of politicians and other VIPs were invited every year. I recalled attending a performance of Mozart's opera *Cosi Fan Tutti* in the East Room of the White House as the guest of Jackie Kennedy, who held the event for the children of ambassadors in Washington. The occasion took place on February 7, 1962 according to the printed invitation, which I've kept together with all the other memorabilia from my Washington days.

I was to work at ICTE for almost thirty years, after further study converting my casual position to a permanent part-time and later full-time position. My early change of direction from an academic career was a fortunate one, because I soon found that I enjoyed teaching much more than doing research. The international students I taught at ICTE were from diverse parts of the world with many from Japan, China, South Korea, Taiwan, Saudi Arabia, and countries in South America as well as some from Europe. Almost without exception, they were interesting and polite, showing respect for their teachers and thus easy and pleasurable to teach.

An advantage of my work at ICTE was for me to quickly become familiar with life in Australia, both in the present and in the past, and with aspects of the English spoken in Australia, including typical Australian expressions and slang, which make it different from other forms of English. Most of the students I taught over the years were learning academic English in order to continue with post-graduate studies at the University of Queensland. They would be living in Australia for a few years, and it was thus important for them to learn about the culture and language of Australia. Although many of the textbooks we used at ICTE came from England or the United States, we always tried to adapt our teaching to the Australian context.

I also taught groups of overseas students who were visiting Brisbane on a short study tour of a few weeks. In addition to classroom lessons, which often included well-known Australian songs such as *Waltzing Matilda*, teachers would accompany these students on day trips to various scenic places around Brisbane such as the Lone Pine Koala Sanctuary, the Gold Coast, or North Stradbroke Island. It was a great opportunity for me to become acquainted with the surroundings of my new home.

23. Guilt

Very soon after my marriage in 1977, my feelings of guilt towards my mother began to resurface. As a young child in Stockholm, I had felt guilty when I didn't behave according to my mother's expectations of how a "good" little girl should behave. My feelings of guilt stemmed from the belief instilled in me while I was growing up that I had to please her, to be what she wanted me to be, to be a dutiful daughter and look after her. If I didn't act in this way, I suffered from guilt.

Now I was again "misbehaving," by living in London away from her. Not having lived at home since the age of fourteen, I never experienced the "teenage rebellion" years. In trying to reach independence and become a person in my own right, I just separated from my mother by moving away from her. Rather than staying with her in Sweden after my parents had retired there, I had chosen to spend a year in Townsville and then get married and move to London with my husband. A little voice in my head kept insisting that I should have stayed in Sweden and have done my duty to look after my aging parents as their only child, and this voice fuelled my feelings of guilt.

Despite my efforts to visit Sweden as often as possible, my feelings of guilt towards my mother worsened after we left England. It had been easy to take the short trip to Sweden from London and take on the role of "dutiful daughter," but not so easy, and very expensive, to visit Sweden from Australia.

My mother also contributed to making me feel guilty by not "letting me go." During the London years, she kept telling me that she could accept us living anywhere away from her, as long as we stayed within Europe. After our move to Brisbane, she wrote: *Wish you at least could have stayed in London.* My father, on the other hand, never made me feel guilty. He had his diplomatic career and, after he retired, he was very involved with his academic research into Turkic languages, which he had been forced to put on hold during his working years in the diplomatic service.

After moving to Brisbane, I also began to connect my feelings of guilt with the punishment my mother had prophesied I would suffer for not behaving according to her expectations, for not acting the way she wanted me to.

"You'll get your punishment one day," she had often told me when I was a young child in Stockholm, and I would never forget those words.

Waiting for this punishment was like waiting for lightning to strike during a severe thunderstorm, or for what I imagine it would have been like to wait for bombs to drop over London during World War II. I remember seeing a movie about a boy on death row in the States who couldn't bear waiting and never knowing when the end would come. He finally committed suicide. I can't remember the title of the movie, but it left a strong impression on me. It felt terrible spending years waiting for my punishment.

In retrospect, I realize that my mother no doubt blurted out her threats that I would be punished one day in anger and frustration when I was misbehaving. She would never have intended that I take her threats seriously, but for many years I did. After arriving in in Brisbane I began to believe that because I had disobeyed my mother by escaping from her and not fulfilling my filial duties towards her, I was to suffer from guilt as my punishment. During my first fifteen years or more in Australia, the way to alleviate this guilt was not only by writing weekly letters to my parents in Sweden, but also by visiting them as often as possible.

My visits to Sweden were, of course, also a way of trying to please my mother. While I was growing up, I spent a lot of time trying to do this, and during the early Brisbane years I was still trying to do so. How difficult it was to succeed in this! No matter how hard I tried, it seemed that she never felt loved enough.

In 1984, soon after we moved to Brisbane from London, my parents decided to come for a visit. I was very excited and spent weeks cleaning and preparing our house in Antill Street and rearranging the rooms in a way I thought would please them. It was necessary to provide them with two separate bedrooms as this was what they were used to. This meant that our almost two-year-old daughter Celia would have to move into our bedroom so that my father could use her bedroom. Then I tidied my study, which would serve as my mother's room, and moved the spare bed from Celia's room to there.

We picked up my parents at the airport and I couldn't wait to show them our first house, where I had done my best to meet their requirements. But after only a short time with us and without any hint of what was coming, my mother turned to me and said: "Mamma doesn't feel welcome." I was too upset to ask what made her say this, but suspected it was because she didn't get my undivided attention, now that I had a husband and daughter to look after.

In early 1988 all four of us were visiting my parents in Stockholm. On January 12 it was my mother's seventy-ninth birthday so I decided to take her out to lunch, followed by a movie to celebrate. It was just the two of us. The movie was *The Last Emperor*, which chronicles the reign of Puyi in China. I paid for a nice lunch at a local restaurant before the film, and as we came out of the theater afterwards, we agreed that the movie had been excellent. Then as we embarked on our short walk back to my parent's apartment on Karlavagen, my mother suddenly turned to me and said, "I don't want to walk with you." She said it abruptly just like that. I felt hurt and angry as I walked away from her and left her to walk home on her own.

A few days later she explained that I should have slowed down, as she was too old to keep up with my fast-walking pace. She was, of course, quite old at the time but fit for her age. She was probably right that I was walking too fast, which is a habit of mine, but it was the way she spoke to me that was upsetting. I had tried so hard to please her, but somehow it was never enough.

On every visit to Sweden, I hoped to be on good terms with my mother, but we always seemed to end up quarrelling and then apologizing in subsequent long-distance letters. It seems clear that there were also feelings of guilt on my mother's part towards me. For example, in September 1990, she wrote: *Often think of you all. A pity I was neither a good mother nor grandmother. I am hoping for a better result next visit.* This refers to us visiting Sweden, not her visiting us in Australia. Did she feel guilty because she hadn't paid enough attention to me while I was growing up, or because she didn't know how to be a good, loving mother, as she herself had never had a loving mother as a role model?

From another letter (from January 1991) it is also evident that my mother felt guilty towards me for leaving me at boarding school so many years ago:

> *Thank you for your letter with all too kind words about your old mother. I am not worthy of all this praise. Forgive me for my many faults. I will, for example, never forget*

when I left Washington (in January 1964) with our dog Ossian and left you behind alone in the school. Of course, I had no choice. I had nowhere to live, and you had no school until the autumn ... I will never forget our conversations the night before our departure! Once again forgive me.

Clearly this departure figured just as greatly in my mother's life as it did in mine!

This is my reply from January 23, 1991:

Everyone has their faults and there is absolutely nothing to forgive! I don't remember any conversations from just before you left Washington. I only remember that Pertti [our chauffeur] drove me to the school.

It's true that I don't remember talking to her before her departure, and I must have totally repressed our parting conversation. It must have been a sad affair because it still preyed upon her mind. I never told her about all the trouble I had dealing with her "abandonment" of me, nor all the anger I had felt towards her. In retrospect, this was foolish of me. Talking about it all might have brought us closer to each other.

I vividly remember how my mother tried to pamper me during the years after I had left home for boarding school and before I moved to Townsville and London. In hindsight, I realize that she was probably trying to alleviate her feelings of guilt for leaving me in Washington. During the summers in Viken, on most mornings she would climb the steep stairs to my bedroom upstairs to bring me coffee in bed.

One day during these years, my mother turned up at my studio apartment at the top of an old apartment building which did not have a lift. (This was when my parents and I were all living in Stockholm after my father's retirement from the foreign office.) When I opened the door to her, she was out of breath, but soon said, "I wanted to see how you were. I just want to take care of you."

I will never forget my answer: "It's too late." This could have been an opportunity to talk about what happened in Washington all those years ago, and today I very much regret my response to her belated attempt to get close to me. At the time, I had only managed to distance myself from her and my feelings of anger had not yet surfaced. My words did have the effect of adding to the guilt I felt towards my mother.

Lillan and Eva, Stockholm, 1975
(copyright Asa Nilsonne)

24. Coping with Two Personae

Eva's two personae

Despite the many positive aspects of living in Brisbane, it became more difficult to balance my two personae than it had been in London. I soon became very busy with two small children and with studying and teaching. Spending many hours per week as a teacher of English, I didn't have the time to teach Swedish as well. Moreover, with Brisbane being spread out over such a vast area, and most Swedes tending to live on the south side of the Brisbane River while we lived on the north, it was time-consuming and complicated to meet Swedish people. Also, I didn't necessarily have a lot in common with Swedes in Brisbane, just because we shared the same nationality. Early on I tried to get to know some Swedes at a Swedish Midsummer celebration, but most of them were homesick and talked the whole time about how much better life was in Sweden. At times I missed Sweden, but I didn't share their feeling of dislocation in Australia. It was a depressing experience that I wasn't in a hurry to repeat.

This left me with little option but to arrange trips to Sweden as often as money and time off work would allow, which was about every one or two years. Sometimes all four of us, my husband and I and our two daughters, would go. Sometimes I would go by myself with one of our daughters. After their only visit to us in Brisbane in 1984, my parents felt they were too old, being in their late seventies, to make any further long flights, and I had to accept this.

I remember how I would switch to my Swedish self and start thinking in Swedish when we reached Singapore and, on the way back, I would again switch in Singapore to my English-speaking self and start thinking in English. All these 24-hour flights were well suited to me, in that I had plenty of time to readjust, even in terms of thinking in a different language.

The other day I happened to come across an email from 2005 from a colleague who commented on this switching between personae:

I hope you had a comfortable trip [to Sweden] *and are now relaxing and catching up with friends and family members. It amazes me when I imagine you switching to your Swedish persona. I have only known your English-speaking side, although of course I realize that we are made up of our lifelong experiences and so in knowing you I know part of your Swedish self.*

I haven't been back to Sweden since the end of 2015, and I sometimes think back to what it was like to switch persona on those trips. It's difficult for me to judge if I was a different person when in Sweden. I know that I would think in Swedish while there, and in English while in Brisbane. I would never translate between the languages in my head when alone. However, I would have to do some translating when my husband or daughters, who only have a limited knowledge of Swedish, were with me in Sweden. One thing I feel sure of is that my English-speaking self was stronger already in the Washington days, and continued to be the dominant part of me after that.

On one of my trips to Sweden with just my husband, I decided to try an experiment. It was the summer of 2010. For a night or two we had booked into the Grand Hotel in Helsingborg, southern Sweden, thinking that we would be given a spacious room perhaps with a view. However, as it turned out, the hotel was fully booked, and our room was quite small and faced a street at the back of the building. It was also very noisy because we arrived on a weekend when an international jazz festival was being held in various places all around the town.

Unable to fall asleep due to the noise, we decided to join in the festival. We were sitting at an outside table under a large umbrella, enjoying the music in the drawn-out Scandinavian twilight and relatively warm weather, when an unknown Swedish couple asked if they could join us as there were extra seats at our table. I decided to pretend I was an Australian tourist with no connection to Sweden. I had no problem convincing them that this was the case until they commented to each other "it's beginning to rain a little" in Swedish and I automatically put my hand outside the umbrella to check if this was true. I was caught out and had to confess. I realized that I could never have been a spy! Clearly there was a fine line between my two personae.

Later during this trip, there was a strange cross-over between my past in Sweden and present life in Australia. The main purpose of our visit was to watch and support my father-in-law, George Corones, who was competing in the World Masters Swimming Championships in Gothenburg. He was in the 90–95-year-old age group. There were not many competitors in this group, but one of them turned out to be my old physics teacher from Sigtuna, Mr. Ferm. It's worth mentioning that George held many world records in swimming, the last one set when he was over a hundred!

During my first twenty-five years or so in Brisbane, I felt I couldn't live fully in the present, but was constantly thinking about my next trip overseas. Yet once in Sweden, I would soon wish I were back in Australia. I felt torn between the two countries. If I went for a walk with my family along the beach at Redcliffe, outside Brisbane, it would start me thinking about the beach in Viken; looking across to Moreton Island would remind me of the view of Denmark from the Swedish coast. If I was taking a walk around Viken and saw a small black dog, I would immediately long for my dog at the time, my little poodle Sasso, at home in Brisbane. Cold, cloudy days in Australia would make me think of typical Swedish summers, whereas unusually hot, sunny days in Sweden would remind me of the semi-tropical climate of Queensland. In both cases I would feel homesick for one of my homes and I could never feel completely happy in either place.

25. Farewells

My mother died in 1999 and my father in 2002. They are buried in the family grave in the old cemetery near Viken's church. During the last ten years of her life, my mother suffered from a number of strokes, which were mild enough for her to continue to live at home in Viken under the care of my father and the excellent home help available in Sweden. Then in February 1999, soon after she had turned 90, a more serious stroke put her in hospital, where she died after a couple of days. I didn't travel from Brisbane to attend the funeral. Her beloved Pekingese, Ming, had been put down a few days before her final stroke, as he was stumbling around and walking into the walls in his old age. Ming had spent most of the day with my mother, and for a while my father worried that the dog's absence had somehow contributed to the stroke. However, medical opinion soon put his fears to rest as there was no evidence that grief could cause a brain hemorrhage.

My father was very protective of me, especially at the end of his life. He was ninety-four, still living at home. He knew he was dying, but he didn't want me to come to Sweden and watch him die, so he didn't tell me.

When I arrived in Viken for his funeral, my aunt told me that she thought it had been the right decision for my father and me. I couldn't have tolerated watching him lying there in pain, and he couldn't have endured seeing my grief. I think he died from prostate cancer, which would have been a fairly long process, but he must have told people not even to tell me this, because I have never been able to have his cause of death confirmed.

My friend Asa (from boarding school and university in Sweden) attended the funerals of both my parents and told me that they were very similar. When I attended my father's funeral in June 2002, I could thus at the same time imagine my mother's service. There were quantities of flowers, the coffin was covered with deep-red roses and lots of people had sent wreaths. Again, there was a violin solo, but played by a different Eastern European soloist. This time the piece was Rimsky-Korsakov's "Hymn to the Sun" from *The Golden Cockerel*. At my mother's funeral the piece had been "Song of India," by the same Russian composer. My parents had been listening to this when they first fell in love as students at Lund University. While my father put a lot of time and thought into my mother's funeral, he was also preparing for his own, no doubt realizing that I was far away and would find it difficult to cope with the arrangements from a distance. It was a very moving service—the first funeral I had ever attended, and the one I had always dreaded the most.

―

Even after my parents were no longer alive, I felt strangely compelled to return to Viken. It was as though I still felt guilty and had to prove I was dutiful. Thus, for a number of years, instead of exploring new countries or new places in Australia, I spent my brief, hard-earned holidays from my teaching position at the University of Queensland visiting old relatives and friends in Sweden. Looking after them in some way made me feel I was continuing to do my duty to my mother.

One of these relatives whom I will always remember is my uncle Bonde. He died at home at the age of 103. My father's sister, Greta, and Bonde had been childhood sweethearts, but when she decided to pursue a nursing career and turned down his marriage proposal, he married someone else. Some thirty years later, after the death of his wife, he and Greta were reunited and married. Bonde was a real connoisseur in the art of living. In retirement, he studied Latin and graduated from the local high school. He also kept up his French at the Alliance Française. He kept fit by taking long walks and bike rides, as well as by swimming all year round in the often-freezing ocean. After my aunt passed away, he moved to a smaller serviced apartment, where he proudly displayed photos of his two wives on the table next to his bed. When I visited him from Australia, we would have dinner in the communal dining room and would then return to his little kitchen for some cheese and biscuits served with red wine. This was a routine he would adhere to even when alone. Bonde is one of my role models.

I also spent a lot of my leave from work being a kind of live-in companion to Karin, a woman in Viken, about twenty-five years older than me. We had often rented her house on previous visits to Sweden while my parents were alive, as their house was too small to accommodate all of us. Gradually Karin and I became close friends. She had been married to the Lutheran priest in Viken who had performed our marriage ceremony. They got a divorce when he left her for another woman, so Karin learned the shoemaking trade in her fifties to support herself. She became the village shoemaker after buying a beautiful old house in the main street which included a shop from which she could work. She continued her trade until she was about eighty. To earn extra money, she also took in boarders during the summer months. Karin lived in her lovely house, managing everything by herself until she died in 2023, just short of her hundredth birthday. I very much admire her independence. She is another one of my role models.

26. Relief

It happened one day towards the end of 2010. As I walked along Gaunt Street in Brisbane towards Newmarket train station, it struck me that I felt happy and could enjoy the present moment to the fullest. As I strolled along, I was conscious of the hundred-year-old timber cottages on my right, shaded by mango trees of the same vintage, and the cooing of doves. When I walked past one of the last houses on my path, I was greeted by Daisy, a black and white border collie, sticking her head out between the palings of the veranda. Every day after this, I continued to walk to the station to take the train to work, and every time that Daisy was out on the veranda, I felt it was a sign that I would have a good day. This feeling of happiness and being alive in the moment has stayed with me.

From this time on, I no longer felt the strong urge to return to Sweden as often as possible, not even to Viken. Thus in 2013, for example, my husband and I spent a very enjoyable holiday in France with only a short stopover at a hotel in southern Sweden. Of course, this lack of urgency to visit Sweden may have been because most of my old relatives, whom I was close to, had died. More importantly, I was relieved to find that I no longer felt guilty about having left my mother in Sweden. But I still didn't understand what had brought about this welcome change in me.

Then, during the process of writing this memoir, I gradually realized a few things which could explain how my feelings of guilt had vanished. First, I stopped believing that my mother had depended so heavily on my visiting her as often as possible. I could now see that after I left Sweden, she would have had a good life in Stockholm and Viken, together with my father and their current Pekingese, seeing many relatives and friends, playing bridge and table tennis, and reading in Swedish, English, and Russian. The famous English novelist, P.G. Wodehouse, creator of Jeeves and Bertie Wooster, once wrote in a letter to his stepdaughter: *All one really needs in life is about two good friends, a regular supply of books, and a Pekingese.* This observation could have been made by my mother.

Lillan with her Pekingese, Mingka, Stockholm, 1978
(copyright Asa Nilsonne)

Next, I no longer believed that she deliberately tried to make me feel guilty because I had moved away from Sweden. I imagine that she just felt sad that I was moving so far away from her and that she would not be able to spend as much time with my husband and me and her two grandchildren as she would have liked. Now that we have a daughter and three grandchildren living in Perth, I can understand how my mother probably felt. I feel sad that I can't see our family on the west coast as often as our daughter and three grandchildren in Brisbane. At the same time, children must be given the chance to lead their own lives, especially after they are married with their own families.

There was also a more important realization, which came to me during the writing process, that helped me to understand why I no longer felt guilty. Although one reason for my leaving Sweden was to escape from my mother's influence over me, and to have the chance to live my own life, it gradually dawned on me that this was not my *main* reason for leaving. In fact, I should have realized much earlier that what I had been trying to do all these years was to cope with having two identities. It would have been very difficult to reach a successful outcome if I had settled in Sweden where my dominant English-speaking persona would not have received its due. This insight brought me an incredible sense of relief and took away the heavy burden of guilt I had been carrying around with me for so many years.

How could I have forgotten all the effort that had gone into keeping my two selves intact? It was easy during the London years, and not only because of the relatively short distance to Sweden. I was living in an English-speaking environment and doing research for my Ph.D. thesis in English literature. At the same time, I had to visit my current supervisor in Sweden from time to time, which I combined with visiting my parents in Stockholm. I also taught Swedish a couple of evenings a week at the Central London Polytechnic. Thus, my Swedish persona was intact too. However, it became more difficult to keep my two identities in balance after we moved to Brisbane. Not having much contact with Swedes, I felt compelled to visit Sweden as often as money and leave from work would allow. My *main* reason for these trips was not, I now realized, to lessen the guilt I felt for leaving my mother. The *main* reason was to maintain my two personae.

In Brisbane I briefly had the chance to get to know and observe two Swedish women who were living here because they had married Australians. Both had grown up in Sweden and had only moved to Australia in their late twenties. While I was still in touch with them, we unfortunately never discussed the problem of a dual identity. However, I suspect that their Swedish personae were much stronger than any Australian side they had acquired. Both of them ended up buying a house in Sweden and retiring there, with an occasional visit back to Brisbane.

For me it was the opposite. Having spent my formative years, aged from seven to fifteen, in the United States, my English-speaking persona quickly became stronger than my Swedish one. In fact, as much as I love Viken, I never really felt at home in Sweden, and can't imagine going back to live there now in my retirement. Despite all my trips to Sweden, my English-speaking persona has gradually grown even stronger, to such an extent that I can now live in the present in Brisbane without any compelling urge to be physically present in Sweden to satisfy my Swedish self.

Of course, this doesn't mean that I won't keep in touch with my Swedish persona in other ways. I still keep in contact by email with many relatives and friends in Sweden. Some of them have visited us in Brisbane, and no doubt I will still make some more trips to Sweden in the future, but probably in combination with seeing some new sights in another country or two. I will also ensure I won't forget my Swedish by reading books in that language from time to time.

27. Becoming Australian

Looking back over the years I have been living in Brisbane, I find it interesting to trace how I have gradually become more and more Australian, adopting an Australian outlook on life and accepting Australian ways. From the early years after my arrival in Brisbane in December 1983, I can recall certain aspects of life that struck me as strange compared to my previous experience, especially from Sweden, but to which I have gradually adapted.

One example of this is the Australian attitude to sport, which to my mind borders on the obsessive and which I found difficult to cope with at first. When my daughter Celia was in grade 5 at Wilston State School, her class entered a competition which they won. The prize was tickets for the whole class to attend a Rugby League football match at Suncorp Stadium, featuring the local team, the Brisbane Broncos. I remember feeling horrified that a bunch of ten-year-olds, even with a teacher supervising them, should be allowed out in the evening to mix with intoxicated rugby enthusiasts. When Channel 7 came to interview the class after their win, they used Celia's comments on the 6 p.m. news: *At first my parents said I couldn't go, but then they said I could,* she said softly while smiling shyly into the camera. I can still remember how angry the other parents were the next day. "Why had Celia been chosen to appear on TV when she (meaning I) clearly hadn't understood what a great opportunity it was to watch the Broncos in person?" I can't say that the years have made me any more interested in Rugby

League, but I can today better understand the parents' reaction. Furthermore, over time I have become increasingly interested in watching sport, especially tennis and even the occasional Rugby Union football match. One major sporting event that I still haven't embraced is the Melbourne Cup. All that dressing up and drinking just for a horse race that lasts only two minutes! After a *7.30 report* program about the mistreatment of the retired racehorses was telecast in 2019, I have an excuse for not watching that race again.

Another obvious aspect of life in Australia which seemed strange to me at first was celebrating Christmas in the summer heat while still adhering to the British tradition of serving hot food. In the past, we usually celebrated Christmas day at Steve's parents' house, where my mother-in-law would prepare a hot meal of ham, turkey, potatoes, and various other boiled vegetables with hot gravy to be poured over the top. Some years we also spent Christmas with them at their beach house where we would still sit down to the same warm food. I was used to the Swedish tradition of celebrating Christmas in the evening of December 24 in a cold climate suited to eating a hot meal. Over the years, we have continued with the Swedish tradition of celebrating on Christmas Eve, which means we can also celebrate with Steve's family the day after. I now find it natural to have Christmas lunch at a beach house in the middle of summer, but we have increasingly moved away from the traditional British food, instead serving cold avocado soup and seafood.

I also found the Australian attitude to work different from the Swedish one. When l lived in Sweden in the 1970s, the term "housewife" was almost a dirty word. At the time. the government was trying to encourage more women to join the workforce and women were indoctrinated into believing they were letting society down if they weren't in full-time employment.

Strongly under the influence of this attitude when I first moved to Brisbane, I immediately started applying for a full-time position as a tutor or lecturer in English at university level, and continued to apply even when I had two daughters under the age of three. I only succeeded in securing casual teaching work, and gradually I realized that the children were more important than a full-time position. I still didn't want to be a housewife but could happily combine staying at home with part-time work and further studies, which would eventually get me a permanent 75 percent position teaching English to overseas students at UQ. This was converted to a full-time position once the girls were at university. This seems a much more sensible approach to work than in Sweden, where most women are still trying to juggle a full-time career and family simultaneously. However, of course I realize that many women in both countries are forced to work full-time to make ends meet when they would rather spend more time at home if they had a choice. Those years, when I could look after Celia and Claire, were some of the happiest in my life. I loved taking them to ballet and tennis lessons, watching them compete in rhythmic gymnastics competitions, arranging birthday parties, and following their academic achievements. Unfortunately, those years seemed to pass all too quickly.

During the many years I worked as a teacher at the University of Queensland, I often noticed a fundamental difference between the behavior of Swedes and Australians. Swedes tend to be very direct, quickly getting to the point and saying exactly what they mean without any introductory words. On the other hand, I noticed that most of my Australian colleagues would usually chat for a few moments on some personal matter before coming out with what they wanted to say. I gradually learned to adopt this approach, making small talk before stating my real purpose. For example, I would say: "Did you have a good weekend? What did you do?" or "I love your dress. Where did you get it?", before asking a colleague if we could discuss some problems one of our mutual students was experiencing. Of course, the Australian way is undoubtedly more polite, but I still found it frustrating and a waste of precious time in a work environment.

When we moved to Brisbane in 1983, it was usual for a married woman in Australia to adopt her husband's surname and give up her own. However, the situation in Sweden was more complicated. In 1920 a law was passed in Sweden which made it mandatory for a woman to take her husband's surname after marriage. In 1963 this law was relaxed, and women had a choice regarding their surname after marriage. Many women decided to keep their maiden name and add on their husband's surname with no hyphen. Thus, they officially had two surnames and could use them together or one at a time, as they chose. For example, I generally use "Jarring" in Sweden but used "Corones" when I was working at UQ. I use both names in my passport and on my Medicare card but must think carefully about other cases. Which name do I go by? I really should try to be more consistent. Women's choice of surnames has more recently become more complicated in Australia too.

I am proud of my two surnames and do not want to give up either of them. Being an only child with two daughters, I don't want the name Jarring to be lost forever in Australia. Thus, Celia and Claire have both been given Jarring as a middle name in the hope that in this way it will live on for at least another generation.

The origin of the name Jarring is also interesting, as I discovered while reading some of my parents' letters. In an early letter before they became engaged, my father wrote to my mother in Lund:

Copenhagen on February 17, 1931

(...) I intend to change my name. Please observe that this is of my own accord and for practical reasons. I must do it before I take out my master's degree. I have waged a hard battle with myself. But I believe I should first try to

persuade my father to change his name so that I don't need to do it. (…) In any case I won't be doing it alone but all the other seven siblings have to agree to it. What do you think? As I said, there is no influence.

In her reply from February 1931, my mother wrote:

(…) How have you suddenly thought of the idea of changing your name? To be sure I very much like the idea but you have always been totally against such "nonsense." What will your name be instead? Or perhaps one isn't allowed to be curious? Good-bye my own beloved. Sleep well and dream of your Lillan.

My father did indeed change his surname and at the same time the surname of his seven younger siblings from Jonsson to Jarring, a taken name with no particular meaning in Swedish and pronounced with an initial "Y" rather than "J" English sound. I assume he wanted a name change, as Jonsson is one of the most common surnames in Sweden whereas Jarring is unusual and only our family have the name. My father took his new surname before he had any idea that he would become a diplomat in the future. It's a strange name for someone in a profession for whom a fundamental requirement is never to strike a *jarring* note. Interestingly, as far as I know, the Press never commented on his name, perhaps because it was considered bad form to do so. After a careful reading of the two letters between my parents quoted above, I am also struck by a feeling that my mother wanted him to change his name before they got married and probably suggested it to him. My mother had the unusual maiden name Charlier, which came to Sweden through a French ancestor in the nineteenth century. I believe names were important to her and she would not have wanted to be one of a multitude of Mrs. Jonssons.

I moved to Brisbane at the end of 1983 but did not become an Australian citizen until March 14, 2002. Prior to this time, the Swedish government did not recognize dual citizenship and I would never have considered giving up my Swedish nationality. The citizenship ceremony took place in Brisbane City Hall with a large number of residents turning up in order to, in unison, make a Pledge of Commitment as a Citizen of the Commonwealth of Australia. There was a choice of two pledges with the first one containing a reference to God, which is the one I chose although I am not a practising Christian. The wording was:

> *From this time forward, under God,*
> *I pledge my loyalty to Australia and its people,*
> *whose democratic beliefs I share,*
> *whose rights and liberties I respect, and*
> *whose laws I will uphold and obey.*

I was happy to finally be able to become an Australian citizen; it didn't feel at all strange. I had been hoping for a long time that Sweden would change its rules, so I was now gaining something important without having to give up my Swedish citizenship in return. Once I became an Australian, I felt even more at home here and became more interested in politics, as I now had a voice through my right to vote.

In this memoir I have been referring to one of my personae as my English-speaking self without distinguishing between the countries where I have been able to cultivate this part of me. The United States, England, and Australia are all English-speaking countries but of course the culture in each is not identical. For me, the eight developmental years I spent as a child in New York and Washington formed the basis of my English-speaking self, but I haven't been back to the United States for many years. Of course, it was interesting and exciting to spend our early married life in London, but I never felt at home in England, even though to some extent living there meant my two personae were in balance. On the other hand, I think I have been lucky to settle in Brisbane. Although Australia shares a history with England and has many of its historical roots there, it is the American aspects of Australia that resonate with me and, to me, outweigh any British characteristics. I can see many similarities between the U.S.A. and Australia. They both have a long history of indigenous inhabitants, who lived in the vast land areas before the countries were settled by Europeans in fairly recent times. Both countries have taken in immigrants from many different parts of the world. There is no obvious class system in either place, unlike in England. The people in both countries are friendly and open. Finally, American customs, which I grew up with, such as the Easter hat parade and Halloween, are now very much part of life in Australia. Living here is the closest I could come to rediscovering my American past and I am happy here.

After my problems dealing with being bi-cultural and bilingual, I was careful to bring up my two daughters, Celia and Claire, as identifying with one country, Australia, and with English as their only native language. This was made easier because my husband Steve does not have any strong ties with Sweden, nor does he speak Swedish. Nonetheless, my daughters do have links with Sweden. They can both understand some Swedish, which they have picked up on various visits. They were both christened in the church in Viken while their grandparents were still alive. They both have dual citizenship, the Swedish one acquired through me as nationality is passed from the mother to the child according to Swedish law. I assume this also means that their children have acquired Swedish citizenship at birth. My daughters also both keep in touch with various relatives and friends in Sweden. However, I am sure they feel totally Australian. Now they are both married to Australians and have happily settled into life in Perth and Brisbane.

28. Never Marry a Diplomat

Once again, I have set up my laptop in the kitchen in our house in Brisbane. I plan to read more of the Lund letters and am eager to find out more about what happened to my parents after the end of World War II. Would I finally understand why my mother warned me never to marry a diplomat? Was she serious in her warning to me?

My parents were stationed in Tehran until December 1945, but during the summer of that year my mother went to Sweden on holiday (her first since 1941). My father wrote the following letter to her in Sweden:

> *Swedish Legation, Tehran July 14, 1945*
>
> *(…) There is talk of me being transferred to Addis Ababa. (…) Just a few days after you left, I was asked if I wanted to go there. I didn't think I could give any other answer than yes as in that case I will be able to open a new legation on my own as chargé d'affaires. I hope you don't feel too sad but that you will be happy in Addis Ababa too.*

Judging by this letter, it seems as though my father didn't consult with my mother before he accepted his new post in Ethiopia. Did she just passively follow him to Addis Ababa, or had they previously come to a joint decision that it was in their best interests for my father to pursue a diplomatic career after World War II, and for my mother to accompany him to wherever they might be posted?

In any case, my parents never returned to their life in Lund or their positions at the University Library.

Instead, they arrived in Addis Ababa on January 5, 1946, traveling directly from Iran. In his memoirs, my father describes how there he was *all alone* (with no other diplomatic staff to help him).

During the first period, Lillan helped me with clerical work, but gradually she became overburdened with other chores.

I assume he is referring to all the diplomatic duties she had to perform as the wife of the chargé d'affaires. From this time on my mother's life changed. Having been in paid work from the age of nineteen and having become increasingly independent and self-confident, my mother would, from this point on, be a diplomatic wife performing unpaid duties all hours of the day and night, and finding herself in an inferior role to her husband. She would never again be in paid employment. She was thirty-seven years old.

My parents were stationed in Addis until the summer of 1948 when they returned to Viken, southern Sweden, for a holiday. After India was granted independence in 1947, there was a need for Sweden to establish diplomatic relations with the newly independent republic. Thus, in September 1948 my parents went by boat to India where my father was to set up a new legation in his role as Minister. It was at this stage that my mother flew home to give birth to me in Sweden in April 1949. Two years later, at the end of September 1951, we flew from India to Tehran where my father had recently been appointed Minister.

In June 1952 we returned to Sweden for my father to take up his role as assistant head of the political section at the Department of Foreign Affairs in Stockholm. The following year he was made head of the section. I found an interesting comment my mother made in a letter from this time in Stockholm. She wrote to my father, who was on a work trip at the United Nations:

It's a pity to not earn any money and I often think of the University Library and the good years in Tehran. However, here in Sweden it's not worth my possibly earning a few hundred kronor as they will of course quickly disappear into tax. I would a thousand times rather be a librarian than an unpaid housemaid in my own house! (September 1955)

During these years in Sweden, it's clear that my mother thought back with longing to her years as a working woman, but realized that it wouldn't be worth her while taking paid work while they were on home soil, due to the tax system in Sweden. My parents would probably have been jointly taxed as a married couple. My father would have had a relatively high salary in Stockholm and any income from my mother would likely have pushed them into a higher tax bracket with ensuing higher tax. My mother also clearly resented the fact that she was forced to do housework, no doubt due to the difficulty and expense of getting help with the household while they were in Sweden.

In May 1956 my father was appointed Ambassador to the United Nations. Then in the late summer of 1958 my parents moved to Washington D.C. for my father to take up his appointment as Ambassador to the United States. They stayed there until January 1964, when he became Sweden's Ambassador to the Soviet Union, a position he held until his retirement from the Foreign Office in October 1973.

At the beginning of this memoir, I discussed some of the unpaid duties Mamma had to perform as the wife of a high-level diplomat. I mentioned the "visits" and "return visits" and the "calling cards" left with the hostess, which were part of the diplomatic protocol she had to follow. I found a letter to my father from 1951 in which she made an interesting comment about the calling cards: *Is it not possible to get a card with both our names on it? These are the ones that should be presented when you pay a visit.* My mother was clearly saying that she should be recognized in her own right and not just as the wife of a diplomat. In his reply my father seemed to be sympathetic to her query: *Unfortunately, I have never ordered any cards with both our names. It's stupid. I guess I will have to do so when I get back home to Sweden.* (November 22, 1951)

I recently found a card with *Mme Lillan Jarring* on the front and a note on the back, sent to me from Moscow. As far as I can recall, nothing was ever done about changing the cards and my mother continued to be referred to as "*Mme. Gunnar Jarring, wife of Sweden's Ambassador*" throughout her years as a diplomatic wife. Perhaps she had a different set of cards printed for her own private use?

During the 1950s and 60s, the view that a woman was inferior to her husband was not just typical of the conservative Department of Foreign Affairs but of society in general. For example, in the first-class passenger list of the M.S. *Kungsholm* from June 1963, my mother was listed as Mme. Gunnar Jarring. Other married women were referred to as Mrs. followed by their husband's first name and surname, or as just Mrs. plus their husband's surname. There was no mention of a married woman's first name, let alone her maiden name.

Having suffered from tuberculosis in her early twenties and endured the painful treatment in the sanatorium for over seven months and for several years afterwards, my mother never fully recovered, and she tired easily. It must have been a strain to be always in the public glare as a diplomat's wife, meeting new people from different countries and different social backgrounds. In the letters to my father, she frequently mentions how much she hated diplomatic cocktail parties from the early days in India right through until the Moscow years, and tried to avoid them if she could. I found several examples of this in the letters she wrote from the mountains in

Mussoorie, where she had gone to escape the extreme heat in Delhi while my father remained in the city for work. (In early May 1950, my mother, the dog Jimmy, and I, together with the current nanny, left for the mountains and remained there until the beginning of October.) When she wrote to my father, Mamma often mentioned how happy she was not to attend the cocktail parties in Delhi. Towards the end of our Mussoorie stay, she emphatically wrote:

> *I am <u>not</u> planning to attend all those never-ending cocktail parties in Delhi but will keep to official functions and lunches and dinners. I really haven't the energy. Even though we have a calm and restful life [in Mussoorie], I am nearly always tired, and I know that things are much more stressful in Delhi.* (26 September 1950)

Standing up for hours on end many nights in a row at these cocktail parties would have been not only physically tiring, but also intellectually frustrating for my mother. Imagine a woman who was very well-educated and used to independent work, having to watch her husband walk off to discuss various complex and interesting political issues with his diplomatic peers, while she had to make small talk with their wives. In another letter from the mountains, my mother made a comment, which seems to indicate that she was thinking along the same lines:

I don't like the atmosphere in Delhi. I don't like the diplomatic wives, except for a few of them. And all these eternal cocktail parties drive one crazy!" (May 24, 1950)

A note my mother included at the back of her diary from 1968 might shed some further light on this situation. In this note she referred to the song: "You'll Find Me at Maxim's," in Lehar's operetta, *The Merry Widow,* and made a short comment that the lyrics provide the "truest" picture of diplomatic life she had come across. The song was sung by Count Danilo, the first secretary at the embassy of a Balkan principality in Paris. He described the life of a diplomat in a facetious manner as consisting of short office hours, drinking alcohol, and having to be diplomatic rather than saying what one really thinks. To take one verse as an example:

> *I'm sitting at my desk by one*
> *Among the urgent files galore*
> *A little furtive drinking done*
> *I'm back at home for drinks at four*

Under the "strain" of it all, Danilo goes off to the famous Paris restaurant, "Chez Maxim," to *lose himself in dreams* and forget about his Fatherland. Was my mother in fact critical of the diplomatic life as being too superficial, with endless cocktail parties and small talk?

In November 1967 my father took up his role as Special Representative of the United Nations Secretary-General to mediate in the Middle East after the Six-Day War in that year. He was still Sweden's Ambassador to the Soviet Union while my mother remained in Moscow for most of the time he was working in his U.N. role.

Thus, during the Moscow years, my mother often performed her role as Ambassadress without the support of the Ambassador. She was able to put her excellent Russian language skills to good use and to work for the embassy in her own right, independently of her husband. While my father was away, she had to keep the residence with its staff running smoothly. She also had to attend and host various diplomatic events as well as visits from Swedish trade delegations, on her own. In her letters from Moscow to my father during these years, she wrote:

> *Everything has gone well, and I've hardly had time to notice your absence. Things have been going non-stop since Sunday. The lunch here was a success. Even [Russian Foreign Minister] Gromyko especially praised the excellent food. (…) Yesterday about 250 people attended the cocktail*

party with very few women among them (30 November 1967)

I love Moscow and would prefer not to move unless it becomes necessary. As we know I in any case have a purpose here. (December 1, 1967)

At the Belochvostikovs I was as usual placed according to your rank and Mrs. Nystrom sat at the end of the table. There is absolutely no difference in my position. (December 19, 1967)

At official lunches and dinners my mother was acknowledged as the wife of the Swedish Ambassador, even in his absence, and treated accordingly. Nystrom kept his secondary position as chargé d'affaires. Belochvostikov was the head of the Scandinavian section of the Russian department of foreign affairs.

Although my mother wasn't paid for her work, I believe that these Moscow years were the high point of her diplomatic life where she could feel useful and appreciated after many years of playing second fiddle to her husband in her role as diplomatic wife. I think she was lucky to have the many years living in Moscow where she could finally once more make use of her many skills and make an important contribution. I admire her for looking after the embassy in Moscow so well while my father was away in his role as United Nations mediator in the Middle East.

It must have been very difficult for my mother to go from being a career woman to taking on her role as diplomatic wife. After being in paid employment, she would have felt she was not sufficiently rewarded for all the unpaid work she did for the Swedish government over many years as the wife of a diplomat. In his memoirs, my father wrote:

During almost ten years in Moscow, Lillan was of invaluable help to me and the Swedish government through her excellent knowledge of Russian. [...] It was a help which, among other things, meant that Russian-speaking guests sitting around the hostess at our table didn't need to feel bored to death because they couldn't communicate with her. Lillan had a knack for in Russian achieving an atmosphere which our guests called "ujutno," pleasant and cozy.

In another place in his memoirs, my father put this idea in even stronger terms:

When in 1973 we had reached the age of retirement from the foreign service, it seemed to me that Lillan, like other wives of ambassadors, should have received a medal, preferably a medal for bravery, for everything she had endured during a long diplomatic life on four continents and for all the unpaid work she had undertaken in some of our biggest embassies. However, my thoughts were not met by any understanding [by the department of foreign affairs] ...

I have now reached the stage where I have finished reading the Lund letters and have used them in many places in this memoir. My manuscript has gone through several versions and my husband Steve has read the drafts and made helpful suggestions for improvement. As is our habit, we are now sitting on our front veranda having an afternoon glass of wine, watching the planes taking off and landing at the airport visible on the horizon. Our miniature labradoodle, Milo, is asleep at our feet after his daily walk.

"Have you seen the Singapore Airlines flight today?" Steve asks as he brings out a bowl of crisps.

"No, it's probably left already," I answer, while thinking how strange it is to see the large plane on an almost daily basis taking the same route from Brisbane to Singapore that I had taken so many times in the past on my way to Sweden.

For several years at this time of day, our topic of conversation has turned to my mother's life and my relationship with her, and it has always been useful to discuss my ideas with Steve. Today I begin by saying, "While I was growing up, I often felt neglected by my mother. At other times, I felt she went to the other extreme and spent too much time trying to bind me to her. She was too possessive and controlling. You knew my mother and have read my manuscript—what do you think about this contradiction?"

Steve thinks for a while before answering. "Well, as a result of contracting TB soon after her marriage and living through World War II, she was forced to wait for many years for the daughter she'd always wanted. When you were born, she had recently given up her work in the library and in Tehran. Having waited so long for your arrival and no longer having a career of her own, you would have become her full-time occupation."

"Yes, you're probably right. I hadn't thought about it like that. It may explain why I felt she was focusing too much on me."

I take a sip of wine and then continue. "The children of diplomats often suffer from being separated from their parents at too early an age. It must be a difficult time for many diplomatic mothers too. In my mother's case, I think it was especially hard because she was too attached to me. I know that she resented that I had to leave home at fourteen and attend boarding schools, first in Washington and then in Sweden, because of my father's diplomatic postings. It would have been difficult for her to 'lose' me when I was still very much a child. I never went through the normal stages of rebellion and moving away from my mother. And she never experienced the stage of gradually letting me go. Instead, there was an abrupt break when I was sent away, which resulted in problems for us both. It took me a long time to fully separate from my mother. Perhaps this only truly occurred when I finally stopped feeling guilty towards her. I hope she finally managed to 'let me go' before her death."

At this point we are interrupted by Milo's insistent barking and whining to take him out for his usual run in the back garden, chasing and fetching his rubber ball. We know it's 4:30 as he's very much a creature of habit.

After ten minutes in the garden, we're back on the veranda and can continue our conversation. "Remember how throughout her life, my mother warned me to never marry a diplomat? Was she being ironic, or did she really mean it? I can't make up my mind. Of course, she loved certain aspects of the diplomatic life. She had excellent language skills which she could put to good use. She met interesting people and lived a life of luxury in many different parts of the world."

"Yes, but what about the drawbacks?" Steve asks.

"Well, as I see it, she didn't want to be *just* a diplomat's wife. In many ways she was a very modern, emancipated woman, who wanted a career of her own. And this was just what the wife of a diplomat was denied."

"True, you had to be generally available and always on duty for your husband's career. I suppose in most cases it's possible for both spouses to have a career, but not in the diplomatic service. This may still be the case today."

We sit silently for a while, lost in thought. Then Steve continues, "Perhaps more than anything, your mother resented the effect the diplomatic life had on her relationship with you. She may have blamed the diplomatic service for destroying the opportunity to have a normal relationship with you while you were growing up."

"I think you're right. And I can take this a step further. I sometimes wonder whether my mother saw my decision to move to England and later Australia as another consequence of her being married to a diplomat. My parents were highly intelligent people, but did they realize that I didn't really feel at home in Sweden, that I felt most at home in an English-speaking environment? They must have been very disappointed that I didn't eventually settle in Viken and raise a family on the spare allotment next to them. I regret that I didn't talk to them about all this."

"So, it seems your mother was serious in her warning to you."

"Yes, when she looked back on her long diplomatic life, she may well have reached the conclusion that she would have preferred a quiet life in Lund with a career of her own in the university library. The position and status of being an ambassadress were a small compensation for not having her own work, for being dependent on her husband, and for not having a normal family life with me at home."

Steve takes a sip of wine and then comments, "She was living in a male-dominated society where it was obvious that her husband's career came first. This must have been a constant source of frustration for her."

Our conversation has come to an end. The wind is coming up and it's getting cold. It's time to give Milo his dinner and to prepare our own. We go inside, closing the door to the veranda and putting the past behind us.

Afterword

In August 2015, I was once again on a visit to Sweden. "Viken's Culture and Village Society" had invited me to unveil a bronze bust of my father, which it had commissioned and financed, and which was sculpted by the Swedish artist Claes Lybeck. The bust was placed outside the building which once housed the post office in the main street. This site was well chosen, because during his retirement my father would visit this old post office almost daily to send his letters to numerous correspondents from all over the world. After the unveiling, there was a lunch for invited guests, which was held in the dining hall of the local primary school, the pupils being away on their summer holidays.

At the end of the lunch and while still seated at our tables, we were treated to a filmed interview with my father from 1999, which was being shown for the first time. In the interview, my father reminisced about his early life in Viken, his school and university days, his life as a diplomat and interesting people he had met in many different parts of the world.

On my return to Brisbane, I was in contact with the interviewer and researcher for the film, Christer Malmstrom, and we decided that I would translate the interview into English. It was subsequently posted with English subtitles on YouTube in 2016 under the title *Gunnar Jarring Reminisces*.[*]

---

[*] https://www.youtube.com/watch?v=Wx2mtlPoIjo

It was during this same visit to Sweden in 2015 that I visited Lund University Library and brought back the letters between my parents on a USB. Translating my father's memories of his early life and later diplomatic service in the filmed interview gave me some new and interesting insights into his life and character, but I felt that there was already so much written about him and by him. In contrast, I knew very little about my mother and was fascinated to get to know her through the letters I had brought back from Lund. My first thought after reading the letters was to write a book focusing on my mother's life and using the letters as support. I wanted to show her in this new very positive light, in which I now saw her. But as I began to write her story, my own life seemed to increasingly emerge. Writing the memoir then became a way to explore my own story as well as my mother's story and to trace our complicated relationship, incorporating the diplomatic framework in which we were both living.

One very satisfying way to stay true to myself and my two personae without moving from Brisbane has been to read and translate into English the hundreds of letters written in Swedish between my parents so that they can be accessible to my husband and daughters in Australia, who don't speak Swedish. The letters are used in many places in this memoir. This translation project has now occupied me for several years. In this way, I have not only been able to actively use my two languages, but I have also reached a much better understanding of my parents and of my mother, in particular. I have gained insights into my mother's true character.

The diplomatic life had a big impact on us both. When my mother found herself married to a diplomat, it came at a great personal cost to her. Having a diplomat for a father involved a cost for me as well. Despite the advantages of the diplomatic life, my mother and I both suffered. This arose not from my father's treatment of us, but from the nature of his work and the demands placed upon him. My mother had to give up having a career of her own and instead had to follow her husband on his diplomatic postings. I had to contend with two main problems as the child of a diplomat: first, living with a kind of dual personality, fully identifying with two different cultures and languages; and, secondly, being forced to be separated from my parents before I felt confident enough to leave the family nest, making my difficult relationship with my mother much worse. Even prior to this separation when I was growing up in the United States, my parents' diplomatic obligations most nights of the week meant that we rarely had meals together or interacted like "normal" families. This may not have mattered so much if I had siblings to keep me company, but as an only child, I grew up often feeling alone and neglected. I didn't have the stable, nurturing childhood which is essential to well-being in later life.

Before I read my mother's letters as well as some of her diaries, preparatory to writing this memoir, my feelings towards her were mainly negative. Even though I was strongly tied to her, I thought she was possessive, manipulative, and vain. I felt she had often neglected me. Perhaps it was easier for me to cope with her "abandonment" of me at the boarding school in Washington if I focused on her negative sides. I didn't appreciate her good qualities or her positive influence on me, but that changed after reading her letters and diaries.

I feel happy that I've come to a better understanding of my mother through writing this memoir. I no longer feel angry that she "abandoned" me by leaving me alone at boarding school in the States nor do I feel guilty because I "abandoned" her by leaving her behind in Sweden while I went to live abroad. I am sorry that I didn't get to know my mother better while she was still alive. With my present understanding of her, and without my previous negative feelings towards her getting in the way, I feel that we could have become good friends. As it was, we unfortunately never became close again after I left home for boarding school and we often argued when I visited Sweden, right up until my last visit the year before she died. Sadly, I'm still left wondering whether she loved me. Perhaps with her background of mostly growing up without a mother, she was incapable of really loving a child of her own. The conclusion I've reached is that she loved me as much as she could love anyone.

My father's case is different. Although when I was growing up, I saw him less often than my mother, I have always felt sure that he loved me. The fact that he was brought up in a stable and loving home environment no doubt made it much easier for him to show his emotions. It didn't seem to matter that I saw less of him because when we were together, we rarely argued. As I was growing up, he was always kind to me and interested in what I was doing. Even though he was a busy man, he made sure that he spent time with me. We were always very close. He provided me with a stable influence, which was a welcome balance to my often difficult relationship with my mother.

Despite the problems I've experienced as the child of a diplomatic upbringing, I've also been fortunate in many ways. There can be no doubt that living in various countries, learning new languages, and meeting many interesting people is not only an advantage but also broadens your life experience and outlook on life.

My mother's warning to me never to marry a diplomat only surfaced in my mind when I embarked on writing this memoir, but it must have been there somewhere in my subconscious, because I was never tempted to marry a diplomat nor to become one myself, for that matter. I would have hated the constant moves from country to country. As the child of a diplomat, I have come off lightly compared to many other diplomatic children, who have moved so often during their childhood that they feel rootless and unable to find a place where they feel they belong. I was lucky to have spent my formative years from the age of seven to fifteen in only two countries, Sweden and the United States. Now, I feel happy to have settled down in one place, Australia, which reminds me of the childhood home to which I felt the strongest attachment, the United States. At the same time, I am sure I will never forget my Swedish roots.

Brisbane, 2024

Acknowledgements

To Brisbane author Melanie Myers:
Thank you for valuable suggestions regarding the structure of my memoir after reading an early draft.

To Swedish author Asa Nilsonne (the Asa who appears in several places in the memoir and who has recently published her own version of life as a diplomatic child: *Den jag blev i Addis Abeba – Who I became in Addis Ababa*):
Thank you for believing in my book and encouraging me to find a publisher.

To my publisher Louis de Vries at Hybrid Publishers, Melbourne:
Thank you for taking a chance on my manuscript.
To my editor Anna Rosner Blay:
Thank you for your excellent editorial work.

Above all, to my husband Stephen Corones:
Thank you for all the discussions we've had over the years about my mother and the story told in my memoir. You could write your own memoir: "Never Marry a Diplomat's Daughter."